Excel

ADVANCED SKILLS

ENGLISH

YEAR 6

AGES 11–12

SPELLING AND VOCABULARY WORKBOOK

Get the Results You Want!

PASCAL PRESS

Kristine Brown

Reprinted 2008, 2009, 2010, 2013, 2014, 2016, 2017, 2019, 2020, 2021, 2022

ISBN 978 1 74125 267 5

Pascal Press
PO Box 250
Glebe NSW 2037
(02) 8585 4050
www.pascalpress.com.au

Publisher: Vivienne Joannou
Series developer: Kristine Brown
Project editor: Mark Dixon
Edited by Mark Dixon
Reviewed by Carolyn Lain and Claire Balaam
Typeset by Grizzly Graphics (Leanne Richters)
Cover and page design by DiZign Pty Ltd
Printed by Vivar Printing/Green Giant Press

Acknowledgements
The publisher wishes to thank the people and organisations who gave their kind permission to reproduce copyright material. Specific acknowledgements appear under each text.

Permission to reproduce extracts from the stories *Where Freedom Is* and *Things in Corners* by Ruth Park courtesy of the copyright owner Kemalde Pty Ltd, c/- Tim Curnow, Literary Agent & Consultant, Sydney.

All efforts have been made to gain permission for the copyright material reproduced in this book, but we have not been successful in contacting all the copyright holders. The publisher welcomes any information that will enable rectification of any reference or credit in subsequent editions.

Contents

To the student

This book is about words: what they mean and how to spell them. It gives you **strategies** to learn new words and lots of **practice** in using these strategies. By the end of the book, you'll feel more confident attempting and learning new spellings and working out the meanings of new words.

Each unit is built around a theme or topic, for example *Let's communicate* and *When things go wrong*. In each unit, you will find ten main sections. You will need a dictionary for some of these, so always have one nearby as you work.

Quick fun

This is a quick puzzle to introduce you to the unit theme. It should give your brain a good workout.

Topic spelling list

The **Topic spelling list** is a list of 22 words related to the unit theme. Some words are easier than others, but you should try to conquer them all. The last two or three words in each list are especially challenging.

Take note of the **Spelling strategy** next to each list. Use the lines provided to write out the words after you have learnt them. Be sure to cover the words up first.

Fill in the gaps

The **Fill in the gaps** activity makes you think about the meanings of the words in the **Topic spelling list.** Only do this activity when you feel confident about the spellings. You will need to look back at the list to choose each word, but once you have chosen it, try to write it in the gap without looking back. This will test your brain a little more—which is good! In some units, you will also find a **Word scramble** to give you extra practice in spelling the topic words.

Killer words

The **Killer words** section contains five or six common words that students of your age often have trouble spelling. It also has some tips for remembering them and one quick activity. These words are not necessarily long, but they are all tricky. You should make a special effort to learn these words now and forever because you *will* need them!

One good idea for tricky words is to write them out in large letters and stick them on your bedroom wall or somewhere you will see them every day. Only take them down when you are absolutely sure that you know them.

Looking at ...

In this section, you will look at an important spelling pattern or rule. In some units, you will look at more than one. Again, it is important to learn the pattern and the words using all the spelling strategies you know.
The activities in this section give you practice in writing the words and thinking about their meaning.

Proofreading

Proofreading gives you a chance to use your spelling knowledge to check someone else's spelling. Try to do it without looking back at the lists.

Vocabulary power

This section looks at different ways to expand your knowledge about words and meanings, and gives you practice in using new words and expressions.

Read and learn

The **Read and learn** section is very important because it gives you practice in expanding your vocabulary in the best way possible—through reading! You might find some of the questions difficult, but that's OK. This section is meant to challenge you.

Puzzle

Here you'll find a puzzle using the words from the unit. You'll find crosswords and wordsearches and sometimes quite 'cryptic' clues (*cryptic* means 'hidden, not obvious').

Your turn to write

Of course, we only need to learn spellings because we need to write. So here is your chance to use the words you have learnt in the unit in a real piece of writing. You'll also be able to use words you have learnt in the **Vocabulary power** section.

Other unit features

You'll also find some other features here and there: **Dictionary search, Do you know this word?** and **Did you know?** Take time to look closely at these. They will broaden your knowledge about the wonderful world of language.

Review units

There are four **Review** units. These will test your spelling of words in the previous five units. You should test yourself and then get someone else to test you—perhaps Mum or Dad.

I hope you enjoy working through the book. Good luck and have fun!

1 Let's communicate!

Quick fun

How many of these **tele**communication words can you complete?

1. T E L E _ _ _ _ _ N
2. T E L E _ _ _ _ E
3. T E L E G _ _ _ H
4. T E L E P _ _ _ Y
5. T E L E C _ _ T
6. T E L E _ _ _ N
7. The word below gives the meaning of ***tele***.
   Can you work it out based on the words above?

   D _ _ T _ _ T

8. What other ***tele*** words do you know?

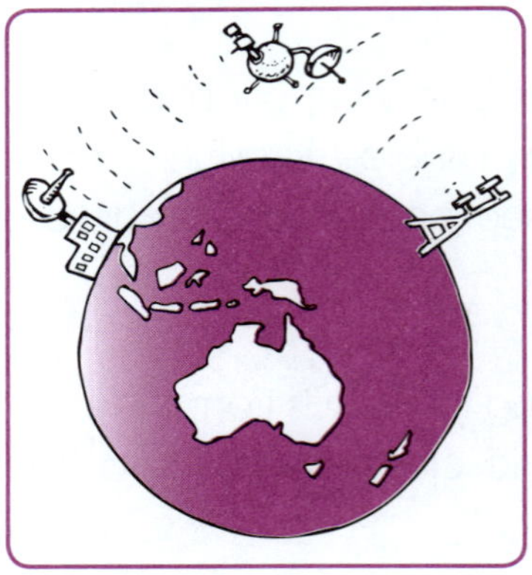

Topic spelling list

email	digital
signal	satellite
text	connection
communicate	technology
communication	receive
conversation	mobile
interactive	language
database	message
download	cyberspace
internet	interpretation
electronic	instantaneously

Super spelling strategy

I'm sure you know the **LOOK-SAY-COVER-WRITE-CHECK** method, but here's a quick reminder:

- **LOOK** hard at the word. Think about the meaning and the spelling pattern.
- **SAY** the word out loud, pronouncing it clearly.
- **COVER** the word up, and **WRITE** it without looking back.
- **CHECK** it. If you get it wrong, use the method again till you get it right.

Try it out now on the words from the **Topic spelling list.** Write them in the line spaces on this page.

Use this space to write out your topic words the first time. Use your own paper for extra practice.

Rewrite here those you had most trouble with.

Fill in the gaps

Fill in the gaps with words from the **Topic spelling list**. Try to write the words without constantly looking back at the spellings.

1. Human beings have used many different methods of ____________ over the centuries.
2. In the very beginning, fire was used to send ____________ across great distances.
3. Although our lives are very different from ancient man, we probably ____________ about similar things—food, shelter, and relationships.
4. Nowadays, ____________ has transformed communication. We can have ____________ across thousands of kilometres using various kinds of telephones and radios.
5. We don't have to use paper and pen to send a letter. Instead we can send a letter in ____________ form using ____________. We can also use ____________ phones to send written ____________. All these methods allow information to be sent and received ____________.
6. In fact, many people now use their phones to send written ____________ messages as much as they use them for spoken conversation.
7. We use the ____________ to find out almost anything we want to know. In addition, we can ____________ information to use when we want to.
8. In the past, we read or listened to learn but now children use ____________ games.
9. Computers allow us to transmit and ____________ complex messages and images across ____________.
10. However, the basic method of communication is still ____________—that is, words. So we still need to know how to read, write, speak and listen well—to ____________ what people really mean.

Killer words

Study these tricky words and tips and then write them without looking back.

listen	Remember the silent ***t***. Learn with *of**t**en*.	____________
listened	You can't hear the ***ed***. Remember it's a past tense form.	____________
answer	Pronounce the ***w*** in your head when spelling: *ans**w**er*.	____________
answered	You can't hear the ***ed***. Remember it is there.	____________
ask	Say it correctly—A-S-K—and you'll spell it correctly.	____________
asked	Again, remember the ***ed*** even though you don't hear it.	____________

Use the **Killer words** in your own sentences. Use at least two words in each sentence.

____

____

Looking at ... *age* words

Many words end with ***age***, e.g. *langu**age*** and *mess**age***. These words can be tricky to spell, because we don't say the vowel clearly and instead say something like ***eh***.

1 Learn these ***age*** words. A good way to remember the last syllable is to say it as the word ***age***.

garbage	passage	sewerage	cottage	mortgage
voyage	usage	shortage	vintage	bandage
storage	stoppage	village	advantage	hostage
package	dosage	courage	damage	savage
cabbage	sausage	manage	luggage	leakage

2 Which words from the box above go best after these adjectives? There might be more than one possibility.

a mysterious ____________________ b smelly ____________________

c dangerous ____________________ d long ____________________

e tasty ____________________ f quaint ____________________

g wrong ____________________ h serious ____________________

3 Which word completes these sentences?

a They had a $100,000 ____________________ on their house.

b The best part of the day was the parade of ____________________ cars.

c The men were held ____________________ until the million-dollar ransom was paid.

d The animal was ____________________ because it had been caged for so long.

4 Do you know these ***age*** words? (They are not in the list above.)

a picture __ __ A G E b electrical measure __ __ __ __ A G E

c save S __ __ __ A G E d bags and possessions __ __ __ __ A G E

e proportion P __ __ __ __ __ __ A G E f drink B __ __ __ __ A G E

g feathers P __ __ __ A G E h hunt for food F __ __ A G E

Proofreading

Can you correct this student's writing? It contains words from all sections of the unit.

I'm glad I live in the 21st century. I can't imagine not having telyphones and televisions and computers in our homes. It would be very boring to write letters every time you wanted to comunicate with someone who was more than a few kilometres away. In films about past times, you sometimes see a person writing a letter, then giving it to someone on horseback to deliver, and then weeks later, recieving the reply from the other person. Nowadays we can send an emale or tecks mesage and get an anser in an instant, or we can just pick up the phone and our words are sent elecktronically down the line. It is so easy to have a convarsation with anyone, anywhere these days. In the past, they also used to send signels from one town to another using flags and different kinds of message machines. Nowadays, we use satelites in space to bounce signles from one country to another—without wire conections at all. Most of us don't really understand how these comunication systems work. We are just glad that they do.

Do you know these idioms?

The phrase ***actions speak louder than words*** means what you do is more important than what you say.

The phrase ***a picture is worth a thousand words*** means people take more notice of pictures than they do of words.

Vocabulary power

There are many precise and interesting verbs to use instead of ***say/said***.

1. Look at the verbs below, and write them under the correct heading. You might write some words under more than one heading. If you are not sure of their meanings, look them up in your dictionary.

state holler sputter observe remark sigh protest announce declare comment contradict stutter mutter roar mumble snap complain sniffle gasp hiss cry insist add blurt whisper screech groan shriek stammer moan bark yell murmur

To say something …

loudly	softly	formally or seriously
angrily	unhappily	nervously
with surprise	about something said or done	against something said or done

2. Choose a suitable word from above to use in these sentences. More than one answer is possible.

   a Henry pointed to his leg and ____________________, 'I can't move. Get help.'

   b Lydia walked onto the stage and solemnly ____________________, 'The winning class is Year 6Y.'

   c Neil ____________________ his comments quietly to himself as the coach droned on and on.

   d 'I didn't do it. I swear,' Cherie ____________________ out suddenly.

   e 'That was a terrific effort, class,' Mrs Soames ____________________ as the children walked from the room.

   f 'I'm too scared to m-move,' Eduardo ____________________.

   g 'Is anyone there?' ____________________ the boys as they made their way through the darkness.

   h 'You traitor,' she ____________________. 'I'll never speak to you again.'

   i 'I didn't do it. How could you think such a thing?' Paula ____________________.

Read and learn

The very best way to expand your vocabulary is to read.

Read the newspaper article below about two very different methods of communication. Take particular notice of the words in **bold**.

Down to the wire, but Morse shows some dash by Richard Macey

It was a technological race between the best that 19th century science could **muster** and the latest in 21st century communications.

Sitting by his Morse code key, set up yesterday inside the Powerhouse Museum, was Gordon Hill, 93, a **veteran** telegraph operator who joined the post office 78 years ago. Across from him, **armed** with the mobile phone, was Brittany Devlin, 13, with two years of texting experience.

The rules were simple. Mr Hill had to translate a message into Morse code and send it to another telegraph veteran, Jack Gibson, 82, sitting a few metres away. Mr Gibson then had to **decode** the transmission and print it out using a **manual** typewriter. Brittany had to use her mobile phone's keypad to punch out the same message, then send it to another phone near Mr Gibson.

Which technology, wondered the crowd of onlookers, was fastest?

The message, a line selected from a teenage magazine, was handed to each competitor: 'Hey girlfriend, you can text all your best pals to tell them where you are going and what you are wearing.'

The race was on. Mr Hill tapped out his message in full, while Brittany **employed** abbreviations to save **vital** time: 'Hey gf you can txt ur best pals 2 tel them where u r going and wot u r wearing.'

Just 90 seconds after Mr Hill began transmitting, Mr Gibson announced he had the message on paper. Brittany's message was delayed somewhere in the **ether** for another 18 seconds.

Three other young competitors challenged the telegraph team and three more times the text messages came in second.

Still, Mr Hill admitted he was impressed by the modern technology, recalling the time in 1961 when he was given an amazing prediction: 'An engineer told me the day would come when we would be able to send messages without wires.'

From the *Sydney Morning Herald*, 15/4/05. Reproduced with permission of Richard Macey.

1 Look back at the way the words **a–h** were used in the article. Then choose the answers that are closest in meaning.

a	muster	**i**	buy	**ii**	use	**iii**	produce
b	veteran	**i**	very old	**ii**	very experienced	**iii**	very clever
c	armed	**i**	equipped	**ii**	holding a weapon	**iii**	holding in hands or arms
d	decode	**i**	read	**ii**	write out	**iii**	translate from code to words
e	manual	**i**	worked by hand	**ii**	book of instructions	**iii**	worked electronically
f	employed	**i**	got a job	**ii**	used	**iii**	attempted
g	vital	**i**	a lot of	**ii**	energetic	**iii**	very important
h	ether	**i**	chemical	**ii**	space	**iii**	museum

2 Newspaper headlines often have more than one meaning. Look again at the headline: *Down to the wire, but Morse shows some dash*.

a The idiom *down to the wire* means 'a close contest'. Why else did the reporter use the word *wire* in the headline? ______________________________

____

b The word *dash* means 'style' or 'excellence'. What other reason did the reporter have for using this word? ____________________

c What does the headline actually tell the readers? Express the meaning in your own words.

____

3 Did you find the results surprising? Why?/Why not?

____

____

____

Did you know?

Language changes constantly. In the past, the word *message* was a noun only, but now because of mobile phones we also use it as a verb, e.g.
She sent me a text ***message***. (noun)
They ***message*** *each other every afternoon*. (verb)

Puzzle

Which words from the **Topic spelling list** hide the words below?

1. A large group. (6 letters) **mob**ile (mob)
2. A kind of pet animal. (11) ____________
3. A word meaning 'say'. (9) ____________
4. A word meaning 'lively'. (11) ____________
5. A word meaning 'an untidy area'. (7) ____________
6. A word for a piece of wood. (10) ____________
7. Another word for information. (8) ____________
8. Another word for lace. (8) ____________
9. A word meaning 'symbol'. (6) ____________
10. A word for a number. (7) ____________
11. A word meaning 'how old'. (8) ____________

Reminder
Use as many words from the unit as you can.

Your turn to write

Think about how communication has changed over the past hundred years. Now think about what might happen over the next hundred years, e.g.

- Will people still use land-line telephones? Mobile phones? The Internet?
- What will they be able to do with them that we can't do now?
- What else might they use?
- Will there be a totally new way of communicating?

Write about your ideas. Be as imaginative as you can. Anything is possible! Remember to revise your writing to check it makes sense, and to check for spelling, punctuation and grammar.

☞ Answers on page 144

2 City streets

Quick fun

Do you know the word METROPOLITAN? It is used to describe anything related to cities and city living. How many words can you make from METROPOLITAN? (There are at least 40.) Give yourself a time limit of 2 minutes or you could be looking all day!

Topic spelling list

- skyscraper
- pedestrian
- congestion
- tunnels
- arcade
- apartment
- suburban
- quay
- convenient
- vibrant
- building
- factories
- facilities
- harbour
- industrial
- commuter
- commercial
- residential
- restaurant
- neighbourhood
- thoroughfare
- accessible

Top tip

Break words into syllables to avoid missing out any letters in longer words, e.g. *RES-I-DEN-TIAL* and *CON-VEN-I-ENT* (one vowel sound per syllable).

Break up the words from the **Topic spelling list** into syllables, and write them out.

Use this space to write out your topic words the first time. Use your own paper for extra practice.

Rewrite here those you had most trouble with.

Fill in the gaps

Fill in the gaps with words from the **Topic spelling list**. You may need to change some endings, e.g. add **s** to words if needed.

1. The __________ closest to the city was filled with narrow streets and alleyways and terrace houses built long ago.
2. The machines of the __________ gradually fell silent as the old __________ area was redeveloped into a recreation zone.
3. The __________ and __________ areas of the city were separated by a wide band of green parkland.
4. In the heart of the city, people mostly lived in small __________ housed in lofty __________.
5. In the __________ areas, they mostly lived in one-storey houses.
6. Some cities make life easier for __________ by closing streets off to traffic.
7. Some cities are lucky enough to be built on wide, deep __________, and many areas are __________ by water as well as land.
8. I love to look at the ferries by the __________ and window-shop in the tiny __________.
9. Life is much more __________ in cities. How on earth do people in the country ever manage day-to-day life without all the __________ of the city?
10. The city may be __________ but because of this, it is also noisy.
11. If you are a daily __________, you depend on the trains and buses being on time.
12. Stanley Street is the main __________, but Camelia Street has the best shops and __________. Jackson Street undoubtedly has the most beautiful old __________.
13. City dwellers have to put up with a lot of __________ on their roads. Many cities these days have created long __________ underneath the surface to make it easier to get around.

Killer words

Study these tricky words and tips and then write them without looking back.

central	It comes from *centre*, but drop the final **e**.	__________
hurrying	A 3-syllable word: don't forget the ***y***.	__________
office	Remember: *I'm* ***off*** *to the* ***off****ice.*	__________
busy	Remember: *bus drivers are* ***bus****y people.*	__________
through	Spell it out loud until you know it. Try to see it in your mind.	__________
accommodation	Remember: ***c****lean* ***c****ute* ***m****arvellous* ***m****otel.*	__________

Can you use all the **Killer words** in one sentence? If you can't manage one, do it in two. Use your own paper.

Looking at … *ant/ent* and *ance/ence* words

Many adjectives end in ***ant*** or ***ent***, e.g. *vibr**ant*** and *conveni**ent***. The vowel sound in these two endings is exactly the same—a bit like an ***eh***. This ***eh*** sound is called a ***schwa*** and occurs in all unstressed syllables.

Adjectives ending in ***ant*** form nouns by changing to ***ance***, e.g. *import**ant*** → *import**ance***.
Adjectives ending in ***ent*** form nouns by changing to ***ence***, e.g. *conveni**ent*** → *conveni**ence***.
A few adjectives change to ***ancy*** or ***ency***, e.g. *vibr**ant*** → *vibr**ancy***.

1 Look up the meanings of any ***ant*** and ***ent*** words below that you don't understand. Then write the noun forms next to each one. Those changing to ***ancy*** or ***ency*** are marked *. Then learn the words and get someone to test you.

ant → ***ance***	***ent*** → ***ence***
brilliant	present
ignorant	dependent
hesitant*	independent
significant	different
abundant	intelligent
elegant	confident
extravagant	persistent
fragrant	consistent*
vacant*	obedient
defiant	excellent
assistant	eloquent
relevant	magnificent

2 Choose an adjective or noun from the lists above to complete these sentences. There may be more than one possibility. You may have to make some words plural.

a She was ______________ she would win. Her marks had been ______________ in all the competitions.

b There was little ______________ between the two cities.

c The temple was truly ______________.

d There was an ______________ of marine animals to be found along the seashore.

e There were no hotel ______________ in the whole city.

f The adults were impressed by the author's ______________ as he spoke to the children.

g Your comment is not at all ______________ to the argument.

h The old lady valued her ______________ and refused to move out of her home.

i The dancers' outfits were simple, but ______________.

j We all understood the ______________ of the principal's announcement—we were in big trouble.

Proofreading

Can you correct the spelling in this student's holiday diary?

15th May

Today we went into London for the first time. We took the train in with all the comuters going to work and school. I was expecting the centrel part of the city to be pretty bizzy, but I couldn't believe just how conjested it was with people and traffic. We had to fight our way along the footpaths of the main throughfares like Oxford Street and Piccadilly. Everyone was hurring, weaving in and out and dashing in front of us to get to taxis or buses. Londoners hardly ever wait for the traffic lights or use the pedestrean crossings; they just leap across the roads whenever they see a break. I don't know how they aren't killed.

I was also expecting lots of skiscrapers and modern bildings, but I was wrong. Most of the bildings were old. Unfortunately, Mum wanted to visit almost every one of them! Dad wanted to visit the nieghborhood where he grew up, so we took the London underground and came out in a place that was very diferent—mostly factorys and big new ofice complexes. Dad was disappointed. He said it was all just a quiet residenshial area when he lived there. After this, we hopped on a double-decker bus and crawled through the streets. We could see everything! It was exellent.

Vocabulary power

Many English words have **Latin or Greek roots**. For example, the word ***ped****estrian* has the Latin root ***ped*** meaning 'foot', the word *metro****pol****itan* has the Latin–Greek root ***pol/polis*** meaning 'citizens/city'.

If you take notice of similarities between words, you will gradually build up your knowledge of common word roots, and this will help you work out the meanings of new words.

1. Do you know these ***ped*** words?
   - **a** A crawling insect. _ _ _ _ _ P E D _
   - **b** A lever worked by the foot. P E D _ _
   - **c** Support for a statue. P E D _ _ _ _ _
   - **d** A light motorcycle. _ _ P E D
   - **e** Get in the way of. _ _ P E D _
   - **f** This measures steps. P E D _ _ _ _ _ _

2. Do you know these ***pol*** words?
   - **a** A plan or course of action. P O L _ _ _
   - **b** Showing good manners. P O L _ _ _
   - **c** A group which keeps order P O L _ _ _
   - **d** One involved in government. P O L _ _ _ _ _ _ _
   - **e** Another word for city. _ _ _ _ _ P O L _ _
   - **f** Belonging to all parts of the world. _ _ _ _ _ P O L _ _ _ _

Do you know this word?

The noun ***urbanisation*** is a word which describes how cities get bigger and bigger as people move away from rural or country areas.

In 1800, only 3% of the world's population lived in cities. In 2000, it had increased to 47%!

Read and learn

Reading stories is an excellent way to expand your vocabulary. Authors use words in interesting ways to create powerful images of everyday things.

Read this story extract. It is about a boy who is staying with his married sister in her flat near Sydney Harbour. He is bored and unhappy, until he finds his way onto the roof of the block.

Take particular notice of the words and expressions in **bold** and think hard about the images they create.

> Gideon lay on his bed, looking out into the gloomy crimson of the western sky. Big planes moved slowly across it, **like gilded blowflies**, already low on their approach to the airport. The sound of the city was a **grinding roar, punctuated by recurrent sudden snarls** as the traffic moved off at green lights.
>
> He thought that there must be a way up to the roof of Cassia Court. He'd have a look at the city with his binoculars, see the names of ships in the Harbour, numbers on planes. Even a flying saucer.
>
> Gideon … rested the binoculars on the parapet. It was freezing cold up on the roof, but interesting. To the south he could see as far as Botany Bay. Maybe as far as Parramatta to the west. He fancied that the **soft smudge of amber fog** lying all along the western skyline came from the industrial suburbs that lay like thirty-two kilometres of solid cement between Sydney and Parramatta. As far as the eye could see, Cassia Court was surrounded by identical, and nearly identical high-rise buildings: **balconied spaghetti packets** called, Gideon imagined, Grevillea Court, Waratah Court, Frangipani Court and so on. At night they looked like **slabs of illuminated honeycomb**, but now they seemed exactly like some vast industrial installation. Nothing to do with humans at all.
>
> Nearby there was nothing to be seen with the binoculars except housewives squeezing kids into pyjamas or getting their husbands' dinners ready.
>
> Away out through the Heads, he picked up a large oil tanker, **small as a log** in those hydrangea-blue waters, tossing up first one end and then the other, and flying what he thought was a Greek flag.
>
> From *Where Freedom Is* by Ruth Park.

1 Choose the correct answer about the images **a–h**. Use your dictionary if you need to.

a What does gilded refer to in **like gilded blowflies**?
- **i** how noisy the planes are **ii** how big the planes are **iii** how shiny the planes are

b What makes a **grinding roar**?
- **i** the traffic **ii** the construction **iii** the people

c What does **punctuated by recurrent sudden snarls** tell you about the noise of the traffic?
- **i** It often increases suddenly. **ii** It builds up slowly. **iii** It is a constant sound.

d What do **roar and snarl** make you imagine the city to be?
- **i** a machine **ii** an animal **iii** a person

e What is the **soft smudge of amber fog**?
- **i** the sunset **ii** the foggy weather **iii** the pollution at sunset

f What does the image **balconied spaghetti packets** refer to?
- **i** short fat buildings **ii** unusual buildings **iii** tall skinny buildings

g The image **slabs of illuminated honeycomb** conveys …
- **i** how the blocks look when the lights are on.
- **ii** how quiet and still the blocks of flats are at night.
- **iii** how the people in the flats are like bees.

h The image **small as a log** emphasises …
- **i** how small the tanker is. **ii** how small the tanker looks. **iii** how strong the tanker is.

2 Look up any other words you do not know.

Puzzle

Can you complete this crossword with words from the unit? **Warning**: a couple of the clues are 'cryptic' (not obvious or clear).

Across

4 An ***ant*** word meaning 'related to'. (8)

5 Sydney has one of these. (7)

6 In the middle. (7)

8 One who walks. (10)

10 Where an officer might work. (6)

11 Great, wonderful, extraordinary. (11)

13 A main passageway. (12)

14 A cute, clean, marvellous motel. (13)

15 Rushing about. (8)

16 *Thorough* without one letter. (7)

18 An area containing residents. (11)

19 Too many cars, too many people! (10)

Down

1 This person travels to the city most days. (8)

2 Lively, bright. (7)

3 Easy. (10)

7 Very clever. (9)

9 The area in which you live. (13)

12 Places you can use for a purpose such as sport. (10)

17 Difficult to spell. Contains a vehicle. (4)

Your turn to write

Reminder
Try to use words from the unit in your description.

Choose one of the following tasks. Use your own paper.

1 Describe a city you have lived in or visited: the landscape, the look of the buildings and streets, and the feel of the city—how busy it is, how friendly, how it makes you feel. OR

2 Imagine your ideal city. Describe it. Use imagery to create a clear picture of the city in your reader's mind. Revise and edit your draft to make sure it expresses your ideas perfectly.

☞ Answers on pages 144–145

3 When I grow up

Quick fun

What's my job?

1. I look deep into people's eyes. _ _ _ _ _ _ _ _ _ _ _ _ _ _
2. I drive, but not on the ground. _ _ _ _ _
3. I manage everything. _ _ _ _ _ _ _
4. Most people call me a chemist. _ _ _ _ _ _ _ _ _ _ _ _ _
5. I write the stories you read each day. _ _ _ _ _ _ _ _ _ _ _ _ _
6. I use a scalpel.
   _ _ _ _ _ _ _
7. I count money (*count* is in my job title).
   _ _ _ _ _ _ _ _ _ _
8. I work at the bar but I don't serve drinks.
   _ _ _ _ _ _ _ _ _

Topic spelling list

career	education
university	ambition
college	casual
degree	permanent
employment	achievement
business	financial
experience	opportunity
future	challenge
qualification	influence
occupation	guidance
apprentice	temporary

Clever clue

There is always *at least one* letter per sound. There may be more than one, but if you put at least one letter for each sound, you'll avoid some common spelling errors, e.g.

temporary not ~~*tempry*~~,
permanent not ~~*perment*~~.

Saying the words out loud in your head as you spell will help you. Use this tip to learn the words from the **Topic spelling list**.

Use this space to write out your topic words the first time. Use your own paper for extra practice.

Rewrite here those you had most trouble with.

Fill in the gaps

Fill in the gaps with words from the **Topic spelling list.** Change word endings where needed.

1. My big brother has a __________ job at the local supermarket while he studies for his university __________.
2. When I grow up I want to start my own __________ like my father. He says it is __________ but very rewarding.
3. It is a good idea to get some voluntary work __________ or part-time __________ when you are in high school.
4. My __________ is to be a primary school teacher, so I will have to go to __________ for a few years.
5. Most people who go overseas get __________ jobs to pay for their travel adventures.
6. To get a good job you need __________ and good __________.
7. I would like to end up in an outdoor __________ like gardening or building.
8. My 17 year-old brother is an __________ carpenter. He studies at __________ three days a week.
9. My grandmother's medical __________ was interrupted by the war.
10. My cousin wants to get a __________ job as a journalist, but he can only find temporary positions.
11. The __________ rewards of a job are not the only thing to consider.
12. The teacher praised her students for their __________ and said she hoped the __________ brought them lots of wonderful __________.

Killer words

Study these tricky words and tips and then write them without looking back.

earn	Remember: *if you* ***learn*** *a lot, you will* ***earn*** *a lot.*	__________
benefit	Say ben-E-fit when spelling.	__________
suitable	Say SU-I-table when spelling.	__________
really	Remember the two **l**s: *real* + *ly* = *really*.	__________
prefer	Learn with *refer* and *referee*.	__________

Unscramble these **Killer words/Topic spelling list** combinations (one word from each list per question).

1. ABLEITUSERCARE __________
2. LEGFREERPCOLE __________
3. BEENFITREEGED __________
4. NEARREFUUT __________
5. YEARLLHENGELCAL __________

Looking at … *ary*, *ory* and *ery* words

The word endings **ary**, **ory** and **ery** are common. The trouble is that they sound exactly the same (the **schwa** sound again—see Unit 2, page 10). There are, however, some patterns to help you:

ary is mostly an adjectival ending, e.g. *tempor***ary**

ery is mostly a noun ending, e.g. *jewell***ery**

ory can be both, but is most common after ***t***, e.g. *labora***tory**.

> **Reminder**
> A **noun** is a naming word, e.g. *job*.
> An **adjective** describes the noun, e.g. *interesting*.

1 Learn these common **ary**, **ery** and **ory** words. Ask Mum or Dad to test you.

ary		ery		ory
temporary	summary	cemetery	misery	satisfactory
imaginary	primary	discovery	bakery	territory
stationary	secondary	machinery	cutlery	laboratory
veterinary	preliminary	mystery	grocery	directory
voluntary	dictionary	scenery	mockery	victory
salary	burglary	stationery	surgery	memory

2 Which of the words above is a synonym for the words below? Use your dictionary if needed.

a	unreal	______________	**b**	not moving	______________
c	yearly wage	______________	**d**	disrespectful humour	______________
e	good enough	______________	**f**	knives and forks	______________
g	papers and cards	______________	**h**	short version	______________
i	unhappiness	______________	**j**	place of research	______________
k	puzzle	______________	**l**	map or list	______________

3 These **ary**, **ery** and **ory** words are not in the list above. Can you work out which word I am thinking of?

a A place to watch the stars. _ _ _ _ _ _ _ _ O R Y

b A place to sleep. _ _ _ _ _ _ O R Y

c A place where artists might work. _ _ _ _ E R Y

d An important blood vessel. _ _ _ E R Y

e A place for plants or babies. _ _ _ _ E R Y

f Unbelievable! _ _ _ _ _ O _ _ _ _ A R Y

g Connected with literature. _ _ _ _ _ A R Y

h What a legend! _ _ _ _ _ _ A R Y

i Celebrating a hundred years. _ _ _ _ _ _ A R Y

j Opposite or argumentative. C _ _ _ _ A R Y

k A place where monks live. _ _ _ _ _ _ E R Y

l Can this person keep a secret? _ _ _ _ _ _ A R Y

Did you know?

The word ***salary*** comes from the Latin word *salarium*. It was the money given to Roman soldiers to buy salt (*salsus*)—a precious item in those days.

Proofreading

Can you correct this student's research assignment about work and study?

I akst my family, friends and nieghbours for one piece of advice they would give to young people about choosing a career. This is what they said:

My Mum: Follow your ambishon. Do something you love.

My Dad: Choose something in which you can acheeve well.

Peter, my neighbor: Do something which chalenjes your brain.

Aunty Julia: You can be successful without going to unversity.

My brother Joe: Eduction — that's the most importent thing. A good job will follow.

My cousin Sasha: Make sure you travel the world but get some qwalications first.

Uncle Vinnie: Start up your own bisness and be your own boss.

Johan, a friend: Take every oportunity you can in life. Never say 'I can't do that.'

Uncle Marko: Do a job which benafits others. The salery is not important.

Vocabulary power

Develop your word power by taking notice of how **word families** are made, e.g. from the verb ***train***, we make:

- two nouns about people: ***train**ee*/***train**er*.
- two nouns about things: ***train**ing*/***train**eeship*.

1 Can you complete the chart with words from the same word family? There may be more than one possibility.

Verb	Noun: person	Noun: thing	Verb	Noun: person	Noun: thing
employ			represent		
study			manage		
assist			earn		
administer			qualify		

2 Nouns are often made with the endings ***hood*** and ***ship***. Use ***hood*** and ***ship*** words to complete the following sentences.

a The ______________***ship*** between the classmates lasted into their adult years.

b My sister got her first teaching position in a small ______________***ship*** on the coast.

c The ______________***ship*** of the athletics club grew rapidly after the joining fee was reduced.

d The young boy showed great ______________***ship*** when his group got lost in the bush.

e There was little ______________***hood*** of the boys beating the visiting team.

f My big brother really enjoys ______________***hood*** now that the baby sleeps through the night.

g Our ______________***hood*** is the best one in the suburb.

h The whole family attended the ______________***ship*** ceremony at the Town Hall.

i Some people believe that ______________***hood*** is the best time of life.

Read and learn

When you read, you often meet words you are not sure of. Take time to look at how these words are used and think about their meaning.

Read Julia's comments about her job as a veterinarian, paying special attention to the words in **bold**.

I work by choice. I also work to earn money as I need to provide for my family. If I suddenly received a **windfall** though, I would still work. So my **motivation** for working is a lot more than money. I work with four other vets in a suburban practice. We mostly treat domestic pets such as dogs, cats and birds, although now and then we have unusual 'patients'. Once we had an albatross which had been found in a park nearby. That was too **exotic** for us, so we sent it off to the zoo for treatment.

I love the challenge of a difficult **diagnosis** and the discussions I have with my **colleagues** as we solve unusual diseases and conditions. The greatest 'low' is when an animal unexpectedly dies after treatment. Sometimes when this happens, the owner's disappointment can turn to anger which is directed at the vet. It can even end up in court. These are the parts of the job I would rather not have to **contend with**, but have to in the course of my work.

I get a lot of variety in my job—in the animals and their problems and the people who bring them in. Our clients come from many different ethnic and economic backgrounds, so there is a wonderful **diversity** in the people I see. In all, I find my work very **fulfilling**.

To be a vet, one has to spend at least four years at university, and although I've always been able to discipline myself to study, I did find it a **grind** at times. When I went to university, the other vet students were almost all male but now they're mostly women. I'm glad I didn't follow the old **stereotype**, as I would have missed out on doing the job I love.

My career ambition at this stage is to be invited to be a partner in a **practice**. It would mean that instead of being an employee, I would become a part owner. I would have more responsibility, but I'd earn more money and it would be more satisfying.

Adapted from *That's a job for me!* by Ross Pearce, Harcourt Brace Jovanovich, 1992. Reproduced with permission.

1 Look back at the way the words **a–k** were used in the text. Then choose the answers closest in meaning.

a	windfall	**i**	pay rise	**ii**	unexpected amount of money	**iii**	prize
b	motivation	**i**	purpose	**ii**	feelings	**iii**	liking
c	exotic	**i**	difficult	**ii**	exciting	**iii**	unusual
d	diagnosis	**i**	discussing a problem	**ii**	identifying the cause of a problem		
e	colleagues	**i**	friends	**ii**	people you work with	**iii**	people at college
f	contend with	**i**	talk about	**ii**	deal with	**iii**	fight
g	diversity	**i**	variety	**ii**	difference	**iii**	liveliness
h	fulfilling	**i**	full	**ii**	satisfying	**iii**	pleasant
i	grind	**i**	very interesting	**ii**	very enjoyable	**iii**	very hard work
j	stereotype	**i**	pattern	**ii**	fixed attitude to something	**iii**	dislike
k	practice	**i**	professional business	**ii**	rehearsal	**iii**	hospital

2 Look up any other words you did not know in your dictionary.

Puzzle

1 Which word am I thinking of?

a **Topic spelling list** word hiding a kind of vehicle. ____________

b **Killer word** hiding a word meaning 'friend'. ____________

c **Topic spelling list** word hiding something to drink out of. ____________

d **Topic spelling list** word hiding a word meaning 'dock' or 'quay'. ____________

e **Killer word** hiding a piece of clothing and a piece of furniture. ____________

f **Killer word** which reveals a palindrome when you take one letter away. ____________

(A palindrome is a word which reads the same backwards and forwards, e.g. *noon*.)

2 Can you work out the following words by playing with words from the unit?

a Change one letter of **college** to get a kind of paper craft. ____________

b Add a letter to the front of **earn** to get a word that might help you do just that. ____________

c Take the first two letters from **casual** and add one to get a word meaning 'normal'. ____________

d Take the first two letters from **degree** and add one to get a word meaning 'think the same way'. ____________

e Take the first two letters from **future** and add two to get a word meaning 'old'. ____________

f Take the first three letters from **university** and add two to get a word meaning 'variety'. ____________

Do you know these words?

Two inventive nouns—***jackaroo*** and ***jillaroo***—describe young men and women who work on sheep or cattle farms in the Australian outback. Can you work out how the words were formed?

Your turn to write

Would you rather be …

1 a brain surgeon or an explorer?

2 a journalist or an accountant?

3 a florist or a hairdresser?

4 a mechanic or a gardener?

5 an actor or a pilot?

6 a jackaroo/jillaroo or a marine biologist?

Choose one pair to write about, and say which you would rather be. You must choose one of the two occupations. You can't say 'neither'! These questions might help you:

- Which job is more interesting?
- Does one job involve travel?
- Which job will pay the most money?
- Is one job dangerous?
- Is one job harder than the other?

Plan your writing and remember to revise it for grammar, punctuation and spelling.

☞Answers on pages 145–146

4 Protecting our wildlife

Quick fun

Can you unscramble the group these animals belong to?

1. MLMAMA ______
2. TEAMIRP ______
3. PETERIL ______
4. BANHIPIAM ______
5. PALRAMIUS ______
6. DICHNARA ______
7. SCUMOLL ______

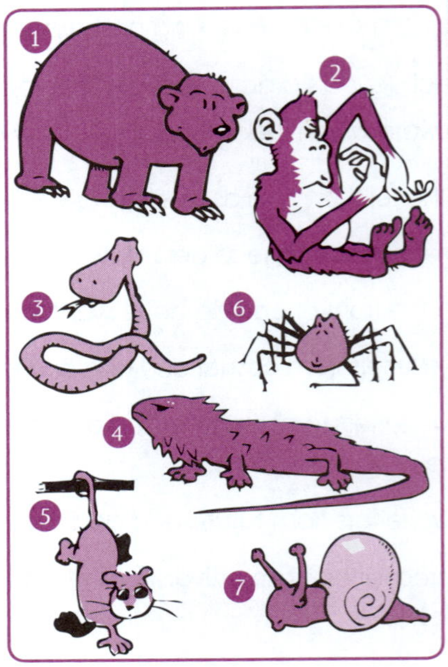

Topic spelling list

destroyed	creature
habitat	unique
survival	territory
species	critically
extinct	discourage
captivity	responsible
poaching	responsibility
disappeared	population
endangered	campaign
threatened	disease
research	ecological

Survival strategy

Be especially careful with past tense verbs. You don't always hear the ***ed*** sound clearly, and so it is easy to miss out the **e**, e.g.

~~destroyd destroid~~ destroyed

~~threatend~~ threatened

~~endangerd endanged~~ endangered

Write out and learn the words from the **Topic spelling list** using all the strategies you know.

Use this space to write out your topic words the first time. Use your own paper for extra practice.

______

Rewrite here those you had most trouble with.

______

Fill in the gaps

Fill in the gaps with words from the **Topic spelling list**. Use your dictionary if you need to.

1. Many animal ________ have become ________ over the history of the planet. Dinosaurs are a good example.
2. Many animals are ________ with extinction but have not yet ________ altogether.
3. The blue whale and Asian elephant are ________ species. This means they have a very high risk of becoming extinct in the near future (about 10–20 years from now).
4. The most endangered species are called ________ endangered. These have an extremely high risk of extinction in the immediate future. An example is the Sumatran tiger.
5. Global warming can badly affect the ________ of some species. For example, it has ________ some of the ________ where polar bears hunt for prey.
6. Many ________ species would be extinct if they were not bred in ________ in zoos around the world. Zoos are also involved in many important ________ programs.
7. When animals are taken illegally and then sold for their skins or bones it is called ________.
8. There has been a worldwide ________ to ________ people from buying ivory products made from elephant tusks.
9. The snow leopard is classified as endangered because its ________ is down to 2500.
10. Domestic animals like dogs and cats can transmit ________ to wild populations.
11. We have a ________ to protect all living ________ on our planet, and the delicate ________ balance. Our own ________ may depend upon it.

Killer words

Study these tricky words and tips and then write them without looking back.

facts	Think of the singular—fact—and add an **s**.	________
lose	Remember *lost* comes from *lose*—so just one **o**.	________
environment	Break into four syllables to hear the middle ***n***.	________
gradually	Break into four syllables to hear the ***u***.	________
example	Sounds like *eggs* but remember it's an **ex** word.	________
being	Say the two syllables clearly: ***be*** + ***ing***.	________

Which **Killer words** are sometimes synonyms for the words below?

1. model ________
2. misplace ________
3. surroundings ________
4. slowly ________
5. data ________
6. a living thing ________

Looking at … homophones

Homophones are words that sound the same (***homo*** means 'same' and ***phone*** means 'sound'), e.g. *preys, prays, praise*.

The lion ***preys*** *on the small deer.* *There was* ***praise*** *for the rangers.* *The farmer* ***prays*** *for rain.*

1 Draw lines to match the homophone to its meaning. Use your dictionary if you're not sure.

a	waist	rubbish	b	dyeing	changing colour
	waste	middle part of the body		dying	stopping living
c	missed	past tense of *miss*	d	coarse	program
	mist	fog		course	rough
e	warn	advise	f	sauce	food dressing
	worn	past tense of *wear*		source	origin
g	alter	table used for worship	h	principal	chief, main
	altar	change		principle	rule, policy
i	strait	direct	j	storey	tale, narrative
	straight	a narrow stretch of water		story	level
k	except	take	l	caught	past tense of *catch*
	accept	but for		court	legal room, sports area
m	mall	claw and bite	n	board	uninterested
	maul	shopping centre		bored	flat, hard piece of wood
o	peace	calm	p	loan	borrowing
	piece	bit, part		lone	single, one
q	idle	inactive	r	profit	someone who predicts the future
	idol	role model, hero		prophet	gain

Did you know?

The noun ***disaster*** comes from ***dis*** + ***aster*** meaning 'star'. It means 'not having a (lucky) star'.

2 These two pairs are not homophones, but they are very close in pronunciation. Draw lines to show which is which.

a	desert	sweet	b	quite	very, rather	c	breath	inhale or exhale (verb)
	dessert	dry land		quiet	silent		breathe	air taken into lungs (noun)

Proofreading

This student got his facts right, but some spellings wrong, in his research assignment. Can you help him to correct them? (Look at the animal spellings as well.)

Some faxs and figures about endangerd speesies:

- There are more than 1000 endangered speces worldwide.
- Some egsamples of endangerd mamals are the African elephent, the right wale and the blue wale, the goriller, the tyger and the giant panda.

- There are 800–1000 pandas including 120 beeng bred in captivty. Populashon growth is graduly destroing their natural habytat: bamboo forests.
- Human beens are the panda's worst enemy. Pochers kill pandas for their skins despite the thret of death or life imprisonment.
- Governments all over the world are doing their best to discurrage poaching of many uneek spiecies. Two men were court in China last month after they captured dozens of wild falcons. Because these birds are so rare, huge prophets can be made by selling them in other countries.
- Some animals are said to be criticly endangered, for exampel there are fewer than 50 mature Asiatic cheetahs alive—all in one single poplation in Iran.
- There are many enviromental organisations which werk hard to protekt our planet's wildlife. They do reserch and run edcation campanes. If we don't want to loose more species in the futore, we should support these organisations.

Vocabulary power

Latin or Greek prefixes at the beginning of a word change the meaning of the base word. The prefix ***dis***- means 'not', or sometimes 'away' or 'apart'. For example: ***dis****courage,* ***dis****agree,* ***dis****appear.*

If you learn the meanings of common prefixes, it will help you work out the meanings of new words you meet. It will also help you spell them so you won't make mistakes like *dissappear* ✗.

1. Can you think of a ***dis*** words for these things?

   a injured DIS __ __ L __ D
   b change appearance DIS __ __ __ SE
   c let down DIS __ P __ __ __ __ T
   d sale price DIS __ __ __ __ T
   e find DIS __ __ __ __ R
   f shame DIS __ __ __ T
   g prove wrong DIS __ __ __ V E
   h drawback DIS __ __ V __ __ __ __ __ E
   i not allowed to compete DIS __ __ __ L __ F __ __ D

2. The words below begin with one of these prefixes: ***sur-*** meaning 'above', e.g. ***sur****vive,* ***dia-*** meaning 'through', e.g. ***dia****meter,* and ***en-*** meaning 'make', e.g. ***en****large*. What are they?

   a A line between the angles of a square or rectangle. DIA __ __ __ __ __
   b Analysis of a medical problem (thinking through). DIA __ __ __ __ __ __
   c Make more wealthy. EN __ __ __ __
   d Above the ground. SUR __ __ __ __
   e Form around a point. EN __ __ __ __ __ __ __
   f Find out, do research. SUR __ __ __

3. Choose three ***dis/dia*** words to use in your own sentences. If you can, make them about wildlife. Use your own paper.

Do you know this word?
An ***ecosystem*** is a community of animals and plants, and their interactions within their environment. An ecosystem can be small—a single log—or large—a whole forest (**eco** means 'house').

Did you know?

Do you recognise these extinct species?

The bird at the top is a **dodo**, a large flightless bird that only lived on one island. (See below.)

The bird underneath is a **moa**, a New Zealand bird eaten to extinction several hundred years ago.

The huge hairy elephant is a woolly **mammoth**, which disappeared about 10 000 years ago.

The bear-like creature with the fur coat is a giant ground **sloth**. It disappeared about 11 000 years ago.

Read and learn

Read this interesting text about the poor old dodo, paying particular attention to the words in **bold**.

In the year 1598, Portuguese sailors landing on the shores of the island of Mauritius discovered a new species of bird, the dodo. Having had no previous contact with humanity, the dodo greeted the new visitors with a child-like innocence. The sailors mistook its lack of fear for stupidity and they **dubbed** the bird *dodo*, meaning a simpleton in the Portuguese **tongue**. Many dodos were killed by the human visitors. Those that survived had to face the animals that were introduced. These dogs and pigs soon became **feral** and by the year 1681, the last dodo had died.

The tragedy of the dodo shows how easy it is for human beings to **disrupt** the delicate balance of an ecosystem by **eradicating** whole species. As one of the earliest examples of **eco-vandalism**, the Portuguese sailors on Mauritius not only wiped out the famous dodo, but disrupted nature in other ways.

Soon after the dodo became extinct, the calvaria tree stopped sprouting seeds and it appeared it would soon face extinction itself. You see, the calvaria tree would only sprout seeds after having been eaten and digested by the dodo.

This story shows why we must work to safeguard the environment. The **bio-diversity** of our world must be protected, for both current and future generations. The dodo was a unique species of bird, that **some** three centuries later is still remembered as a symbol of the harm humankind can do. As the memory of the dodo lives on, we must not forget to **take heed of** such a warning—particularly as more and more species are brought to the point of extinction.

1. Choose the answers that are closest in meaning to the way the words **a–i** are used in the text.

a dubbed	i described	ii called	iii laughed
b tongue	i pronunciation	ii language	iii translation
c feral	i wild	ii hungry	iii predatory
d disrupt	i improve	ii disturb	iii divide
e eradicating	i killing off	ii taking care of	iii eating
f eco-vandalism	i ignoring the environment	ii wrecking the environment	
g bio-diversity	i variety of living things	ii biology	iii differences
h some	i a few	ii approximately	iii a little
i take heed of	i pay attention to	ii take action	iii react to

2. Look up any other words you did not know. You might also like to look for more information about the dodo or other extinct animals.

Puzzle

See how you go with this crossword. The words can come from any section of the unit.

Across

5. Misplace, not win. (4)
8. Extremely. (10)
10. Opposite of *encourage*. (10)
11. Natural environment. (7)
13. Basic unit of animal and plant classification. (7)
15. Was under threat. (10)
17. Everything around us. (11)
18. A kind of research. Begins with a prefix meaning 'over'. (6)
19. A person who hunts or kills animals illegally. (7)
20. Part of the verb *be*. (5)

Down

1. Sounds sweet, but is really a very dry area. (6)
2. Little by little, bit by bit. (9)
3. Opposite of *appeared*. (11)
4. Said to be true. (5)
6. Not existing any more. (7)
7. Totally wrecked. (9)
9. A course of action. (8)
12. Land or region. (9)
14. Means and rhymes with 'sample'. (7)
16. One and only. (6)

Reminder
You can find this kind of information on the Internet. Some websites are devoted to just one animal, e.g. the International Rhino Foundation. Others cover many, e.g. the WWF.

Your turn to write

Find out 5–10 facts about an endangered animal you are interested in, e.g.

- What is the population now?
- Why are they in danger?
- Where is their natural habitat?
- What is being done to protect them?
- Are there any captive breeding programs?

Then choose one of the following tasks. Plan your writing and revise your draft well to be sure it makes sense.

1. Write a short report about the animal. OR
2. Write a letter to your student council (or another group) arguing that you should raise money for the protection of the animal.

☞ Answers on pages 146–147

5 For and against

Quick fun

What is your opinion on these questions? Just a one or two-word quick answer will do.

Should students wear school uniforms? ____________________

Do violent TV shows and films make people more violent, less violent or have no effect?

____

What is the most important thing kids can do to protect the environment?

____

Who would you confide in if you had a problem?____________________

Do you think most children your age would agree with you? On page 31, you can check what children in America thought.

Topic spelling list

oppose	opinion
prove	doubt
evidence	issue
rarely	certainly
balance	suppose
completely	absolutely
disadvantage	serious
decide	various
reason	definitely
argument	neutral
believe	controversial

Advantageous aid

When adding endings, think of the base word and don't drop letters or change them without a good reason, e.g. *definitely* = *definite* + ***ly***.

Learn the words from the **Topic spelling list** and write them out. Be particularly careful with the ***ly*** words.

Use this space to write out your topic words the first time. Use your own paper for extra practice.

Rewrite here those you had most trouble with.

Fill in the gaps

Fill in the gaps with words from the **Topic spelling list**. Change word endings where necessary.

1. Yesterday in class, we discussed the __________ of violence on TV.
2. In a debate, the speakers have to give good __________ for their __________. They also have to __________ (or *rebut*) the other team's case.
3. Sometimes you have to argue for the side you don't even __________ in. Also, you can't be __________—that is, having no opinion either way.
4. Petra and Vin are really good at finding factual __________, but it's not always possible to __________ your point with facts.
5. Our last class debate was about city and country living. Our team talked about __________ negative aspects of city living like pollution and traffic.
6. Everyone laughed when Charlie said that one __________ of city living was being squashed on trains and buses.
7. Our teacher, Ms Pell, said that it was good to use humour but she wanted us to make __________ points as well.
8. Our class has had one debate against 6M and there was no doubt about it: we were __________ thrashed. Their team were __________ better than us.
9. I often get to be first speaker, but I __________ get the chance to be third speaker because Tamana is so good at rebutting the other team's __________.
10. Today Ms Pell is __________ who to put into a debate against Lydell Primary. I hope she picks me because the topic is reality TV. I __________ we will win because they are the regional champions. Our last debate with them was on the __________ issue of cloning.

Killer words

Study these tricky words and tips and then write them without looking back.

actually	Four syllables, not three. Say them out loud.	__________
usually	Same as above. Learn the two words together.	__________
generally	Four syllables. Say it out loud to remember the middle **e**.	__________
always	Learn these three ***al*** words together:	__________
almost	*all* always drops an ***l*** when it's a prefix.	__________
already		__________

Can you put all of the **Killer words** into the paragraph below so that it makes sense? (Use each word only once.)

__________, I'm __________ __________ on time for school, but Lola __________ beats me. She's __________ in the playground __________ or in the classroom talking to Ms Pell.

Looking at ... *able* and *ible* words

Adjectives ending in ***able*** and ***ible*** can be tricky because you can't hear if the vowel is an ***a*** or an ***i***. (It's the *schwa* again!). Always check the dictionary when in doubt. If you have to guess, go for ***able***—it's more common than ***ible***.

Note: some ***able***/***ible*** adjectives can be changed to adverbs and nouns, e.g.
prob**able** ⟶ prob**ably** ⟶ prob**ability**   poss**ible** ⟶ poss**ibly** ⟶ poss**ibility**.

1 Learn these ***able*** and ***ible*** words and choose one to match each meaning given below.
Note: word roots ending in **e** drop the **e** before adding ***ible*** or ***able***, e.g. *sense* ⟶ *sens**ible***).

able		*ible*	
probable	believable	possible	legible
improbable	available	impossible	edible
suitable	valuable	eligible	flexible
reasonable	lovable	sensible	terrible
advisable	comfortable	invisible	horrible
capable	reliable	responsible	incredible
miserable	desirable	audible	irresistible

a can be eaten ______ **b** hard to believe ______
c able to compete ______ **d** ready to be used ______
e unlikely ______ **f** wanted ______
g very unhappy ______ **h** appropriate ______
i very able ______ **j** can be depended on ______
k can move/bend ______ **l** able to be heard ______
m able to be read ______ **n** attractive ______
o reasonable ______ **p** recommended ______

2 Cover up the words and fill in the missing vowels. Write them out both ways to see which one looks right.

a PROB __ BLE **b** BELIEV __ BLE **c** VALU __ BLE **d** COMFORT __ BLE
e IMPOSS __ BLE **f** INVIS __ BLE **g** TERR __ BLE **h** HORR __ BLE
i RESPONS __ BLE **j** REASON __ BLE

Word scramble

Which words from the **Topic spelling list** and **Killer words** are scrambled below?

1 SATMOL ______ 2 TUBDO ______
3 LULUSAY ______ 4 REALRY ______
5 CABLEAN ______ 6 CIDEDE ______
7 RISAVOU ______ 8 SESPOPU ______

Proofreading

Can you correct these students' debating drafts? They are on opposite sides of the debate on *City living is better than country living*.

Milo

My team will proove to you that there are many more bennefits to living in the country. Kira will talk about the piece and tranquility of the country compard with the conjestion and polution of the city. She will also talk about the advanteges of beeng close to nature and the enviroment. Jay will tell you about his own experences living in the country and this real life evidance is sure to perswade you. Without doutt, by the end of this debait, you will have disided that we are correct. Like us, you will want to move to a country town tomorrow.

Matilda

In my opinon, it is certenly better to live in the city than the country. I will give you three very convincing reesons. Firstly it is so much more conveniant. You can reach theatres and sports stadiums and museums and galleries very quickly and easily. Secondly, the city is definitly more exciting and vibrent. Every time you walk on the street, you see something interesting. Thirdly, there is genrally more oportunity for education and emploiment. Allmost all the jobs are in the big citys. I supose if you live in the country you might disagree with me. To be honest, I realey enjoy visiting the country but I know that on ballance I perfer to live in the city.

Vocabulary power

Next time you're writing on the computer, highlight a word and then go to the thesaurus (usually in the *Tools* menu). You'll see synonyms for your word—but no meanings.

Have you ever used a **thesaurus**? A thesaurus is a book which groups words of similar meanings. For example, if you look up ***doubt*** in the *Macquarie Junior Thesaurus*, you will find these words listed with it: ***distrust, disbelieve, question, query*** and ***take with a grain of salt***. You'll also find the exact meaning of each word and an example of how it is used.

1. If you have the *Macquarie Junior Thesaurus*, look up ***doubt*** now and read the five word entries. If you have a different thesaurus, use it to look up ***doubt***, and write down the words given.

   ____

2. Now use your thesaurus to look up these words. Write down three synonyms you find.

   a debate ________ ________ ________

   b choice ________ ________ ________

   c usual ________ ________ ________

   d various ________ ________ ________

   e reasonable ________ ________ ________

3. Choose one synonym for each word above to use in a sentence. (Try to use words you have not used before, but don't use ones you don't understand.)

Read and learn

Always try to use your own experience as well as the context to work out the meanings of new words.

I am sure you have watched reality TV at some time and have an opinion about it. Read the following opinions, paying special attention to the words in **bold**.

- Some people believe that reality TV is just a passing **fad**, but I disagree—I think it's here to stay.
- I have to watch reality TV or I would **be out of the loop** when I talk to my friends the next day.
- I get totally **engrossed** in these shows. I have to follow them through to the end.
- I don't like the 'every man for himself' **mentality**. What happened to cooperation and friendship?
- I am **appalled** by the disgusting behaviour of some contestants.
- I don't like the way the contestants have to betray **allies** in order to win, but it makes it interesting.
- There will always be some bad programs, but I believe the **genre** itself will last.
- I think the popularity of reality TV will **dwindle** fast when suddenly there is nothing else to watch.
- In my opinion, some shows **promote** very poor values—even cruelty towards others.
- I like to watch teams **vying** for the big prize. It's very educational about human nature.

1. Choose the answers that are closest in meaning to the words from the text **a–j**.

a	fad	**i** competition	**ii** idea	**iii** fashion
b	be out of the loop	**i** be ignored	**ii** be laughed at	**iii** be unable to take part
c	engrossed	**i** involved	**ii** enraged	**iii** bored
d	mentality	**i** mindlessness	**ii** attitude	**iii** value
e	appalled	**i** horrified	**ii** annoyed	**iii** puzzled
f	allies	**i** enemies	**ii** contestants	**iii** friends
g	genre	**i** program type	**ii** popularity	**iii** content
h	dwindle	**i** explode	**ii** increase	**iii** shrink
i	promote	**i** encourage	**ii** sell	**iii** typify
j	vying	**i** looking	**ii** competing	**iii** working

2. Look up any other words you didn't know in your dictionary.

Do you know this word?

The adjective ***ambivalent*** means you can't make up your mind on an issue, e.g.

*I'm **ambivalent** about reality TV. I can see its bad points, but I think it has some good points too.*

Puzzle

How many of the words from the unit can you find in the grid below? (There are 20.)

D	I	S	A	D	V	A	N	T	A	G	E	U	J	A	K
E	S	H	B	C	G	C	A	W	O	E	O	S	Q	R	V
C	S	B	S	B	V	T	C	U	N	N	P	U	Y	G	A
I	U	M	O	T	N	U	C	D	Y	E	I	A	L	U	R
D	E	X	L	Z	L	A	P	R	A	R	E	L	Y	M	I
E	O	G	U	B	U	L	R	I	D	A	R	L	S	E	O
P	M	A	T	K	F	Y	O	J	H	L	E	Y	R	N	U
Z	H	F	E	F	E	Y	V	D	X	L	F	G	B	T	S
I	S	T	L	A	L	R	E	A	D	Y	M	F	A	B	O
A	J	I	Y	U	T	S	X	E	K	L	D	P	L	B	O
N	D	V	O	H	A	L	W	A	Y	S	V	E	A	E	P
C	O	M	P	L	E	T	E	L	Y	N	K	Q	N	L	P
P	U	R	U	S	X	B	Q	C	R	H	T	W	C	I	O
B	B	Y	J	Q	L	W	S	U	P	P	O	S	E	E	S
F	T	A	V	Y	K	A	C	G	J	M	D	I	Z	V	E
E	M	W	Z	D	E	F	I	N	I	T	E	L	Y	E	X

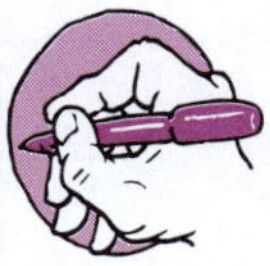

Your turn to write

Choose one of the following tasks.

1. Write your opinion on one of the topics mentioned in this unit, such as school uniforms, violence on TV, city and country living, reality TV, etc.
   - Begin by stating your overall opinion (e.g. *In my opinion … , I believe …*)
   - Then give three reasons why you think this way (e.g. *Firstly … secondly … thirdly/lastly …*)

OR

2. Imagine you are about to debate the topic *Reality TV is bad for us.*
   Write three points for each side of the argument.
   Remember to check your writing carefully for spelling, grammar and punctuation.

Quick fun: response to survey questions

Who to confide in? Mum 51%; Dad 16.6%; brother 7.9%; sister 7.9%, grandparent 4.4%, other 11.2% (includes friends, cousins, aunts, uncles and pets).

School uniforms? 72% no; 28% yes.

Effect of violent shows? Make people more violent 40%; less violent 10%; have no effect 50%.

Most important thing kids can do for the environment? Recycle 35%; buy environmentally-friendly products 16%; write to politicians 5%; raise money for causes 16%; plant trees 20%.

☞ Answers on pages 147–148

Review 1

Now let's see what you remember of the words you learnt in Units 1–5. There are four tests in this review. You could do all in one session, or you could break them up and do them over a few days.

Step 1 Look at each group of words in the test to revise the spellings.

Step 2 Cover the five words up and test yourself (column 2). Try to do all five words in one go.

Step 3 Write your score out of 5 in the box. If you got any words wrong, go back and study them again.

Step 4 If possible, ask someone to test you on the words later—an hour or even a day later (column 3).

Test 1

Study	Test yourself	Test with another person
communication satellite conversation database signal	/5	/5
digital technology interpretation language message	/5	/5
listened text sausage asked damage	/5	/5
cyberspace receive voyage answered passage	/5	/5
pedestrians tunnels suburban convenient facilities	/5	/5
harbour commuter thoroughfare commercial ignorant	/5	/5
	Total score = out of 30	Total score = out of 30

Test 2

Study	Test yourself	Test with another person
central hurrying busy confident through	/5	/5
accommodation brilliant excellent pedestrian neighbourhood	/5	/5
significant career university college achievement	/5	/5
intelligent office experience future ambition	/5	/5
magnificent temporary casual permanent imaginary	/5	/5
financial opportunity degree challenge voluntary	/5	/5
	Total score = out of 30	Total score = out of 30

Test 3

Study	Test yourself	Test with another person
earn benefit suitable really prefer	/5	/5
summary preliminary memory cemetery destroyed	/5	/5
machinery mystery scenery satisfactory survival	/5	/5
species extinct captivity disappeared campaign	/5	/5
endangered threatened creature unique ecological	/5	/5
discourage research population facts lose	/5	/5
	Total score = out of 30	Total score = out of 30

Which word?

1. Don't ______________________ paper. (*waist, waste*)
2. It's ______________________ simple if you think about it. (*quiet, quite*)
3. I have to ______________________ him before it's too late. (*warn, worn*)

Test 4

Study	Test yourself	Test with another person
environment gradually example being believe	/5	/5
prove rarely balance decide opinion	/5	/5
doubt issue certainly definitely suppose	/5	/5
absolutely serious neutral actually capable	/5	/5
generally always incredible already sensible	/5	/5
usually available comfortable terrible horrible	/5	/5
	Total score = out of 30	Total score = out of 30

4 Put some ______________ on it and it will taste better. (*source, sauce*)

5 He was lost in the ______________ for weeks. (*dessert, desert*)

6 They crossed the narrow ______________ in a small canoe. (*strait, straight*)

7 I ______________ the award on behalf of the class. (*except, accept*)

8 Mum said she wanted some ______________ (*piece, peace*)

Well done. That's a lot of words you know how to spell!

☞ Answers on page 148

6 Ancient civilisations

Quick fun

Ancient Egyptian writing used hieroglyphics: simple pictures to mean words or sounds, e.g. *Cleopatra* was written  .

Can you use our hieroglyphics to work out these very old jokes?

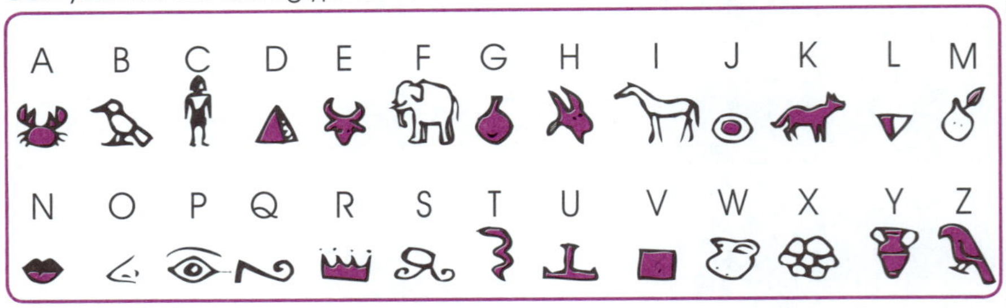

1 What was a popular dance style in an ancient Egyptian disco?

_ _ _ _   _ _ _ _ _ _ _

2 What do you call a holiday taken by a dead pharaoh?

_   _ _ _ _ _ _ _ _ _ _ _ _ _

Use this space to write out your topic words the first time. Use your own paper for extra practice.

Topic spelling list

bronze
pyramid
tomb
reign
burial
secret
sacred
site
ancient
statue
palace

treasure
excavation
decipher
pharaoh
jewellery
religious
worship
sacrifice
embalming
archaeology
hieroglyphics

Deadly strategy

Be on the lookout for homophones when spelling and think about meaning as you write, e.g. *reign* (rule) and *rain* (water), *site* (place) and *sight* (seeing).

Learn the words from the **Topic spelling list** using all the strategies you know and write them out in the space provided.

Rewrite here those you had most trouble with.

Fill in the gaps

Fill in the gaps with words from the **Topic spelling list**. Change the endings where necessary.

1. ____________________ is the study of buildings and objects, usually buried, which show us how past civilizations lived.
2. ____________________ Egyptian writing uses more than 2000 ____________________ characters each representing a common object such as a bird, cup or basket.
3. In an attempt to preserve their bodies forever, Egyptian kings (called ____________________) had massive ____________________ built for themselves and their families. An elaborate process called ____________________ was used to stop their bodies decaying.
4. Archaeologists have found out a great deal about the ____________________ beliefs and ways of ____________________ of past peoples from objects left in tombs and shrines.
5. The ancient Egyptians built large stone ____________________ as temples or ____________________ chambers.
6. ____________________ over the last few centuries has unearthed weapons, furniture, vases and ____________________ made of ____________________, silver and gold, and musical instruments.
7. Many scholars have worked hard to ____________________ the symbols and writings of past civilisations in India, China, Egypt and other parts of the world.
8. Many pyramids in ancient Egypt had ____________________ passages and chambers in which great treasures were stored.
9. Unfortunately, over the centuries, some wonderful ____________________ from ancient times have been stolen by people who only wanted to make their own fortune.
10. When new temples were built, ____________________ were made to the gods. These sometimes involved the killing of animals or even humans.

Killer words

Study these tricky words and tips and then write them without looking back.

eventually	You'll remember the ***t*** if you think of *even**t***.	____________________
during	Say clearly with a ***d*** and you'll get it right.	____________________
early	Remember: put your ***ear*** to the clock to be ***ear**ly*.	____________________
calendar	Use a spelling pronunciation: *cal-end-AR* **(*ah*)**.	____________________
conquer	You'll remember the ***qu*** (***kw***) if you think of *con**qu**est*.	____________________
period	You'll remember the ***od*** if you think of *peri**od**ic*.	____________________

Which **Killer words** mean something like ...

1. in the middle of? ____________________
2. beat? ____________________
3. in the end? ____________________
4. length of time? ____________________
5. before time? ____________________
6. schedule? ____________________

Looking at … *ph* words

Some common words have **ph** for a **f** sound, e.g. *deci***ph***er* and ***ph****araoh*. Many of these words are of Greek origin.

1 Learn these **ph** words and look up the meanings of any words you don't know. Look out for patterns.

phrase	phony	nephew	microphone	telegraph
phase	dolphin	alphabet	phonetic	graphic
sphere	pheasant	orphan	pharmacy	triumph
graph	trophy	physical	photograph	catastrophe
geography	cellophane	physique	phobia	apostrophe

2 Which words from the list have the following meanings?

a prize ____________ **b** fake ____________

c a large bird ____________ **d** victory ____________

e disaster ____________ **f** body shape ____________

g development stage ____________ **h** a few words ____________

i fear ____________ **j** visual ____________

3 Which words might you see in a book about …

a the planet Earth? ____________

b inventions? ____________

c language? ____________

4 Make up four **true** and **interesting** sentences using ***ph*** words in this section. Use your own paper.

Proofreading

Can you check the spelling in this student's research report?

Some interesting faxs about anchent Egypt

- The Egyptian civilsation grew up along the banks of the River Nile. In fact, Egypt ockupied allmost the same area as it does today.
- People's personal possessions were berried with them. Furniture and other household items, jewlery and even food have all been found preserved in tooms.
- People also took images of some animals to their graves as offerings to the gods.
- Cobras, vultures, hawks, bulls, crocodiles and cats, for egsample, were considerd sarced and wershiped in elaborate religius festivals and ceremonies.
- These animals were given proper burialls to please the gods. Many animal cemeteries have been exvacated and found to contain mummified cats, dogs, birds and baboons.
- Egyptians beleived they could comunicate with the gods threw the king. The king was thought to be so holy that he could not be referred to directly. Instead he was called 'great house', or in Egyptian *per-o*. From this, we get the word *pharaoh*.

Vocabulary power

The English language often takes words from **foreign languages**. Sometimes these words are used and spelt the same way as they were in the original language, e.g. *pharaoh* for an Egyptian king.

Sometimes their meanings and spellings change. An example is ***caravan***, which comes from the Persian ***karvan***. This word originally meant a company of people traveling across the desert, but now it usually means a live-in van we might use for holidays.

Draw lines to match the foreign words below with their English meanings. Use your dictionary if needed.

Word	Meaning in English
bazaar **(Arabic)**	A race around poles and obstacles on skis or in boats.
mosque **(Arabic)**	A wooden frame to hold a picture as it is painted.
zombie **(African)**	A variety of food set out for you to choose from.
icon **(Russian)**	Take things into or out of a place illegally.
slalom **(Scandinavian)**	A sports event consisting of boat races.
smorgasbord **(Scand.)**	A person brought back to life by magic; a person acting like the walking dead.
easel **(Dutch)**	A poor city area where one racial or social group live closely together.
smuggle **(Dutch)**	A holy painting; a famous person who is very special; a computer symbol.
regatta **(Italian)**	A small pretty cave.
ghetto **(Italian)**	Someone who does risky, dangerous and perhaps criminal things.
grotto **(Italian)**	A large, often destructive, sea wave caused by an underground earthquake.
karaoke **(Japanese)**	A marketplace or event like a fete.
tsunami **(Japanese)**	A building for Islamic worship.
desperado **(Spanish)**	Singing along with a recording of popular songs for public entertainment.

Note: some very common English words are foreign borrowings. Did you know that ***hamburger*** and ***noodle*** are from German, ***pyjamas*** and ***shampoo*** are from Hindi, ***piano*** and ***umbrella*** are from Italian, and ***mosquito*** and ***guitar*** are from Spanish?

Do you know this word?

A ***dynasty*** is a family of rulers or a period during which they rule, e.g. *Egypt was ruled by 31* ***dynasties*** *over 3000 years*.

Dictionary search

Look in your dictionary for the precise meanings of these interesting words and jot them down.

1. phantom ______________________
2. philosopher ______________________
3. phoenix ______________________
4. phenomenon ______________________
5. phantasmagorical ______________________
6. prophet ______________________

Read and learn

When researching school assignments, you will often meet new words. Always try to make a sensible guess at their meanings before using the dictionary or asking for help. Read the text below, taking special notice of the words in **bold**.

The next world

The ancient Egyptians believed very strongly in life after death, which they referred to as 'the next world'. They believed that eternal life could be ensured by respect for the gods, preservation of the body by mummification, and certain burial and funeral **rites**.

When a person died, he or she was thought to go through a series of **ordeals** which have been **depicted** in some detail in ancient wall paintings. The dead person had some assistance to deal with the journey: *The Book of the Dead*, which contained spells, a map and information to help **bypass** certain dangers, and various **amulets** to ward off any danger met along the way.

First, the dead person had to persuade the old ferryman, Aken, to take him or her across the River of Death in his little papyrus boat. Then he or she had to pass through the Twelve Gates, each guarded by a fire-spitting serpent and a guardian **deity**, often with the head of an animal.

The next task was to **confront** a panel of judges, who read out a list of sins and **misdeeds**. The dead person had to swear innocence to each of these. If the dead person passed this test, he or she entered the Judgement Hall of Osiris, ruler of the Kingdom of the Dead.

Then came the most challenging ordeal: the **deceased**'s heart was weighed against the Feather of Truth. If the heart outweighed the feather, it was believed that the deceased had a heart made heavy with evil deeds. Then Ammit, a god with a crocodile's head and a hippopotamus's legs, would **devour** the heart, and so condemn the person to eternal **oblivion**. If the feather outweighed the heart, it meant the person had led a **virtuous** life, and he or she could join his ancestors in the afterlife.

The ancient Egyptians believed that, in the afterlife, the dead person continued the occupations of his or her life. This explains the various **artefacts**, such as writing materials, clothing, wigs, perfume, make-up, furniture and tools found in excavated tombs. The Egyptians even provided the dead with food for the afterlife. They placed food near the body and also drew food on the tomb walls. They believed that these drawings would be transformed into real food if the real food ran out.

1 Choose the answers that are closest to the meaning of each word **a–m** as it is used in the text.

a	rites	i	right way to do something	ii	set of actions and words		
b	ordeals	i	trials	ii	orders	iii	pains
c	depicted	i	described	ii	pictured	iii	detailed
d	bypass	i	go around	ii	walk past	iii	fight against
e	amulets	i	objects worn to protect	ii	jewels	iii	ammunition
f	deity	i	vicious animal	ii	god or goddess	iii	security guard
g	confront	i	fight	ii	face	iii	argue with
h	misdeeds	i	mistakes	ii	names	iii	bad acts
i	deceased	i	dead person	ii	god or goddess	iii	sinner
j	devour	i	eat	ii	destroy	iii	use
k	oblivion	i	being forgotten	ii	suffering	iii	happiness
l	virtuous	i	happy	ii	long	iii	good
m	artefacts	i	interesting artworks	ii	objects made for a particular purpose		

2 Look up any other words you did not know in your dictionary.

Puzzle

Across

4 Beat or win. (7)
6 Hidden. (6)
8 A place fit for a king or queen. (6)
9 Connected with religion. (9)
11 An offering to a god. (9)
12 A massive stone structure built as a tomb. (7)
15 In the end. (10)
17 Change one letter of *warship* to get a word meaning 'honour'. (7)
18 Not always made of jewels. (9)
19 A carving of a human or animal. (6)
20 Better ________ than late. (5)

Down

1 Very, very old. (7)
2 A metal combining copper and tin. (6)
3 You'll be rich if you dig this up. (8)
5 A length of time. (6)
7 Something to help you track time. (8)
10 Place of excavation. (4)
14 Holy. (6)
16 The noun from the verb *bury*. (6)

Your turn to write

Imagine you are an archaeologist working on an excavation site in Egypt, where the tomb of an ancient king or queen has been discovered. Write a letter or email back home to your family, telling them about the discovery, and the kinds of things you have found. Use your imagination!

Use the words and information in this unit. If you want, look up more information about, for example:

costumes	jewellery and cosmetics	burial procedures
gods and goddesses	wall paintings	hieroglyphics
food	furniture	pyramids

Remember to plan your writing before you start and to revise carefully.

☞Answers on pages 148–149

7 Book review

Quick fun

Can you match these well-known children's books to the places featured in the stories? You might want to ask a family member or friend to help you.

The Wind in the Willows	Middle Earth
The Wizard of Oz	Never-Never Land
Alice's Adventures in Wonderland	Narnia
	Toad Hall
The Adventures of Robin Hood	Crunchem Hall Primary School
Hating Alison Ashley	London
Lord of the Rings	Sherwood Forest
Oliver Twist	The rabbit hole
Matilda	Emerald City
The Lion, the Witch and the Wardrobe	Barranga East Primary
Peter Pan	

Topic spelling list

tension	character
description	humour
style	humorous
series	atmosphere
author	fantasy
popular	theme
suspense	adventure
mystery	illustration
dialogue	thoroughly
genre	fascinating
hilarious	intriguing

Fantastical hint

When you're not sure of a word, write it out two or three different ways to see which way looks right. Often you'll recognise the correct spelling when you see it: ~~exiting~~ *exciting* ~~exsiting~~.

Learn the words from the **Topic spelling list** and write them out.

Use the 'try it out' strategy if you need to.

Use this space to write out your topic words the first time. Use your own paper for extra practice.

Rewrite here those you had most trouble with.

Fill in the gaps

Fill in the gaps with words from the **Topic spelling list**. Change the endings if needed, e.g. make them plural.

1. The ____________ in some books is so unrealistic, but in others it is exactly like real life.
2. Have you read all the books in *The Deltora Quest* ____________ by Emily Rodda? I really like her ____________ of writing.
3. Who is your favourite ____________, and what is your favourite ____________: fantasy, adventure, mystery or something else?
4. Graeme Base's ____________ in *Animalia*, *The Eleventh Hour* and *The Sign of the Seahorse* have been made into fantastic jigsaws.
5. I like books that are action-packed and full of ____________ ____________, the Lemony Snickett *Series of Unfortunate Events*, for example.
6. The main ____________ of *Boss of the Pool* are friendship and trust.
7. I get really scared when I read ____________, but at the same time I ____________ enjoy being scared.
8. The author created a threatening ____________ with the descriptions of the wind and rain.
9. The Harry Potter books are one of the most ____________ children's books of all time, selling over 260 million copies so far. The wonderful ____________ are heroes to a generation of children.
10. My brother only reads ____________ novels. He says it is ____________ to be transported to other worlds and times. He's not interested in real-life stories at all.
11. The ____________ built as the villain got closer and closer to the unsuspecting children. Then Mr Knight stopped reading, leaving us all in ____________ till tomorrow.
12. There is a lot of ____________ in some old classics like *Alice in Wonderland* and *Winnie the Pooh*. My little sister thinks *Winnie the Pooh* is absolutely ____________.

Killer words

Study these tricky words and tips and then write them without looking back.

favourite	Think of ***our*** *fav**our**ite*.	____________
recommend	Think of ***m**any* ***m**arvellous* books to get the double ***m***.	____________
though	Spell it out loud until you know it!	____________
enjoyable	Think of *enjo**y*** and you won't forget the ***y***.	____________
strength	Stretch the word out to get those final sounds: *N-G-TH*.	____________
beginning	Three ***n***s to remember.	____________

Try to use all the **Killer words** in one sentence. It's possible, but if you're stuck, you can use two.

____

____

Looking at … *ous*, *ious* and *eous* words

Many adjectives end in ***ous*** e.g. *humor**ous***. Others end in ***ious***, e.g. *hilar**ious***, or ***eous***, e.g. *courag**eous***. The ***eous*** spelling is not so common and often occurs after ***g*** or ***n***. Always check the dictionary if in doubt.

1 Learn the words below and look up the meaning of those you are not sure of. Ask Mum or Dad to test you when you're ready.

ous		*ious*	*eous*
humorous	famous	hilarious	courageous
dangerous	nervous	curious	gorgeous
generous	adventurous	obvious	hideous
enormous	marvellous	various	courteous
glamorous	ridiculous	devious	spontaneous
ludicrous	unanimous	obnoxious	simultaneous

2 Which of the words above could you use to describe these people or situations? (There may be more than one possibility.)

a A very tall basketball player. ______________________

b The answer to a simple puzzle. ______________________

c A beautiful model. ______________________

d A child who constantly asks 'why?'. ______________________

e An Antarctic explorer. ______________________

f The voting in a class election. ______________________

g A person who donates to charity. ______________________

h A person waiting for exam results. ______________________

i An ogre in a fairy tale. ______________________

j A very funny joke. ______________________

3 Which of the words from the list mean the same as the phrases below?

a horrible, revolting ______________

b tricky, deceitful ______________

c at the same time ______________

d natural, without thought ______________

e absurdly funny ______________

f wonderful, extraordinary ______________

g many, different ______________

h polite, respectful ______________

Proofreading

Can you check the spelling in this book review? Remember to look for words from previous units too.

My favurit book when I was little was *Fantastic Mr Fox* by Roald Dahl, definitly one of the most brillient authers on the planet. In fact, it is still one of my top five books even thogh I am now 12. *Fantastic Mr Fox* tells the story of the crafty, wily Mr Fox and three farmers, Boggis, Bunce and Bean: 'about as nasty and mean as any men you could meet'. The three farmers set out to get Mr Fox but they are no match for his cunning and devous mind. Not only is the story hilairious, but the illstrations by Quentin Blake are just marvellos. As well as the four main karacters, we meet Mrs Fox and their four children, who all help to outwit the horable, obnoxus farmers.

I supose I would say this classic book is most suitibel for children aged about 5 or 6, but reely I would reccemend it to all ages. It has everything: aventure, suspence, tenshun, great dialog and wonderful langwige. Once you start reading, it is imposible to put down. The book makes you respect how animals manaj to servive the nasty things humans do to them. However, I don't think this is a sierous messaje. The book is really just fantastic fun.

Vocabulary power

There are many excellent words to use to talk or write about **books**. You should try to use them in your reviews instead of always using the same words, e.g. *good, interesting, boring, funny*, etc.

1 Read through this terrific collection of words. Then write each word next to the general meaning below.

intriguing witty original thrilling action-packed tedious
humorous fine zany
enjoyable moving outstanding amusing dull comical
tense wacky surprising gripping weird
fascinating tragic hilarious frightening
fast-paced bizarre
monotonous predictable
spooky authentic genuine
depressing realistic terrifying
un-put-down-able enthralling excellent nail-biting

good ____________________

interesting ____________________

unusual ____________________

exciting ____________________

boring ____________________

funny ____________________

sad ____________________

real ____________________

scary ____________________

2 Now write three **true** sentences about books you have read using some of the words above. Try to include some words from the **Looking at** … section.

Read and learn

Read the reviews below, taking special notice of the words in **bold**.

Two great books for *Deltora Quest* fans

How to Draw Deltora Monsters by Marc McBride, Scholastic, 2004

Emily Rodda's *Deltora Quest* series has been one of the most popular children's book series in recent years. A wonderful feature of the series has been the delightful cover illustrations of the talented Marc McBride. Now McBride offers young fans an **insight** into how his pictures have been created, with a step-by-step guide to drawing the **fantastical** creatures from the series. As well as dragons, there is the fearsome knight Gorl, the gentle muddlers, the slug-like Glus, the vicious Vraal and more.

Detailed instructions for each beast begin with basic shapes which are then built on until the beast is complete and ready for colour. Variations in **posture** and action are suggested, along with tips to make the illustration complete.

How to Draw Deltora Monsters will delight Deltora fans, especially those already **endowed** with artistic talents. The detail of the original illustrations means that their **recreation** is not simple, even with McBride's detailed instructions. That said, the book holds interest even for those (like this reviewer) too **awed** to even attempt the drawing exercises, as a fascinating look at the process of creating true masterpieces.

Tales of Deltora by Emily Rodda, illustrated by Marc McBride, Scholastic, 2005

This book of tales contains the secret history of Deltora. That is a **startling** claim, I know, but it is true. With these words, Josef, the Palace librarian, begins this magnificent volume, a **boon** for fans of the Deltora Quest series. Presented in large format hard cover, this is a collector's item which provides the history of Deltora **prior to** the events of the fifteen books of the Deltora Quest series.

There are nineteen tales here, providing recounting Adin's adventures as he collected the gems to make the Belt of Deltora. Each story is **self-contained**, but best enjoyed in order, as the plot builds on previous tales.

Do you know this word?

A ***stereotype*** is a fixed idea about a group of people, such as males/females and cultural groups, e.g. *The heroines in most fairy tales fit the female* ***stereotype****: quiet, beautiful and passive.*

This history is gorgeously **complemented** by full colour **plates** illustrated by Marc McBride. Filled with dragons and other mythical creatures of Deltora, each is finely detailed and **lavishly** coloured. Fans of the Deltora series will be delighted with this new offering. Those who've not yet read the series will be **inspired** to do so.

1 Choose the meaning that is closest to the words **a–n** as used in the reviews.

a	insight	**i**	understanding	**ii**	vision	**iii**	inner meaning
b	fantastical	**i**	great	**ii**	unusual	**iii**	imaginary
c	posture	**i**	position	**ii**	picture	**iii**	attitude
d	endowed	**i**	lucky	**ii**	provided	**iii**	able
e	recreation	**i**	remaking	**ii**	leisure	**iii**	drawing
f	awed	**i**	impressed	**ii**	awful	**iii**	untalented
g	startling	**i**	frightening	**ii**	shocking	**iii**	surprising
h	boon	**i**	blessing	**ii**	surprise	**iii**	disappointment
i	prior to	**i**	before	**ii**	after	**iii**	at the same time
j	self-contained	**i**	happy	**ii**	complete	**iii**	sequential

k complemented — i said something nice — ii matched and made better
l plates — i things to eat from — ii full-page illustrations — iii writing
m lavishly — i elaborately — ii lightly — iii nicely
n inspired — i influenced — ii interested — iii asking

2 Look up any other words you did not know.

Puzzle

Which words from the unit am I thinking of?

1 Contains a **farmyard enclosure** for pigs. _ _ _ _ _ _

2 Contains a **number** between 1 and 10. _ _ _ _ _ _

3 Change the first letter to get **a piece of gossip**. _ _ _ _ _ _ _

4 Contains something to keep you **cool**. _ _ _ _ _ _ _ _

5 Ends with the opposite of **you**. _ _ _ _ _ _

6 Contains a 3-letter word meaning '**belonging to us**'. _ _ _ _ _ _ _ _ _ _

7 Ends with a 4-letter word meaning '**repair**'. _ _ _ _ _ _ _ _ _ _

8 Past tense of **think** without the ***t***. _ _ _ _ _ _ _

9 An ***ous*** word containing **anger**. _ _ _ _ _ _ _ _ _ _

10 The adjective from **vary**. _ _ _ _ _ _ _ _

11 The noun from **suspend**. _ _ _ _ _ _ _ _ _

12 An anagram of **green** (rearrange letters to get a new word). _ _ _ _ _

13 An ***ous*** word containing a place to play **tennis**. _ _ _ _ _ _ _ _ _ _

14 Which word from the **Topic spelling list** contains all five vowels? ____________________

Your turn to write

Check out a few websites like aussiereviews.com (www.aussiereviews.com). They will give you good ideas about books to read, and about how to write reviews.

Review one of your favourite books. It can be fiction or non-fiction, funny or serious, poetry or prose, or anything at all.

Follow this basic structure:

- the title, author, type of book
- the general topic or theme
- the main events of the plot and main characters (don't tell the whole story in detail)
- comments on the author's style, illustrations, etc.
- your overall opinion and recommendation.

Remember to revise and edit carefully to make your writing as good as it can possibly be.

☞ Answers on page 149

8 How do you feel?

Quick fun

Do you know what *emoticons* are? The word *emoticons* comes from *emotion* + *icons*, and describes the symbols people use as shortcuts when writing text messages and emails.

Can you draw lines to match these 'face' emoticons to their meanings? To help you, **:** (a colon) represents the eyes, – (a hyphen) represents the nose, and **( )** (brackets) represent the mouth.

happy	:O	embarrassed	:–<
angry	:–)	very sad	;–S
surprised	:–(	only joking	:–$
sad	:–||	confused	;–)

Topic spelling list

calm
proud
contented
irritated
annoyed
frightened
anxious
curious
surprised
cheerful
rather
worried
jealous
confident
disappointed
determined
emotional
sincere
comfortable
self-esteem
embarrassed
devastated

Sensational strategy

A good trick for spelling difficult words is to invent a 'spelling pronunciation'. When learning these words, say them exactly as they are spelled, e.g. say *COM-FORT-ABLE* and *FRIGHT-EN-ED*.

Learn the words from the **Topic spelling list** using spelling pronunciations when needed.

Use this space to write out your topic words the first time. Use your own paper for extra practice.

Rewrite here those you had most trouble with.

Fill in the gaps

Fill in the gaps with words from the **Topic spelling list**. You might need to add endings such as ***ly*** or ***ed***.

1. I was so __________ when I found out I had worn different coloured socks onto the stage. I was __________ with myself for being so careless.
2. Jake seemed __________ sorry for his behaviour, but unfortunately Kenny seemed __________ not to forgive him.
3. We were very __________ that the school fete had to be cancelled because of the rain. However, we became more __________ when we were told the school had to close for a week because the river had flooded.
4. Mum always thinks of what can go wrong when I go away on camps—snake bites, bee stings, broken bones, sunstroke—you name it, she's __________ about it. She also gets __________ when the time comes to get on the bus.
5. We were rather __________ but very __________ when we heard our school had won the poetry competition.
6. Marion is always __________ of her cousin. She wants everything her cousin has, including her friends.
7. I used to get very __________ in front of a crowd of people but I'm getting a bit more __________ in public nowadays.
8. Joanna was quite __________ immediately after the accident but she became rather __________ when the paramedics said she would have to go to hospital.
9. We found the cat sleeping __________ at the end of the bed, purring __________.
10. My little sister is __________ about absolutely everything. She drives Mum and Dad mad with endless questions.

Killer words

Study these tricky words and tips and then write them without looking back.

who's	Only use if you can replace it with *who is* or *who has*.	__________
whose	About possession: *whose pencil*? (the pencil of who).	__________
scared	No double ***r:*** *scarred* means 'having a scar'.	__________
laugh	Just chant it or write it out till you remember it.	__________
thought	Learn with *ought*, *nought* and *bought*.	__________
pleasant	Think of *please*, drop the **e** and add ***ant***.	__________

Can you use all the **Killer words** in one sentence? If not one, try it in two.

____

____

Looking at … *ive* words

Many adjectives end in ***ive***, but the sound is more like **eh** + ***v***. (As explained in earlier units, this **eh** sound is called a *schwa*, and it can be tricky to spell.)

Tip: English words never end in ***v***, so if you hear a ***v*** at the end, add an ***e***.

1. Learn these ***ive*** words. Use your dictionary if in doubt about any meanings. (Take notice of any common word patterns.)

active	imaginative	descriptive	decisive	sensitive
passive	repulsive	impressive	explosive	relative
massive	impulsive	excessive	abusive	narrataive
talkative	competitive	possessive	offensive	inquisitive
appreciative	secretive	aggressive	apprehensive	persuasive

2. Complete the boxes with ***ive*** words from the list above to describe these people.

a Joey never keeps quiet. ______________________

b Freddy likes to win. ______________________

c Jenna is always asking 'why?'. ______________________

d Van feels things strongly. ______________________

e Trina can make a decision. ______________________

f Nina is good at debating. ______________________

g Josh likes a fight. ______________________

h Petra plays a lot of sport. ______________________

i Mala does things without thinking first. ______________________

j Yolanta writes fantastic stories. ______________________

k Harry fears many things. ______________________

l Hamed is good at everything! ______________________

3. Now make up some **true** sentences about your friends using ***ive*** words. Be very kind, won't you!

____

____

4. Which ***ive*** words from the list mean the same as these words?

a too much ______________ **b** a story ______________

c a family member ______________ **d** huge ______________

e hideous ______________ **f** insulting ______________

Proofreading

Can you correct the spelling mistakes in this student's unit test? Note: there are a few tricky words from the last two units also. Write the corrections in the spaces.

carm ______________ rather ______________ fasinating ______________

proude	______	wurried	______	laugh	______
contented	______	jealous	______	imagative	______
chearful	______	disapointed	______	thought	______
confidant	______	determind	______	pleasant	______
persuasiv	______	emotional	______	talkativ	______
comftable	______	secretive	______	serprised	______
frightend	______	sincere	______	impressive	______
curous	______	embarased	______	hilairious	______
enjoiable	______	ankshous	______	strenth	______
annoyed	______	jewellery	______	irritated	______

Vocabulary power

Antonyms are opposites, e.g. ***happy*** and ***sad, bored*** and ***interested***. Sometimes there is more than one antonym for a word.

Do you know these words?

An ***introverted*** person is one who is shy and enjoys being alone (from Latin = 'turned inward').

An ***extroverted*** person enjoys being with others (from Latin = 'turned outward').

1. Draw lines between the antonym pairs in the circle below. All are useful adjectives to describe people's feelings or behaviour. Use your dictionary if you need to.

joyful foolish proud enthusiastic accidental humble graceful courteous generous stupid intentional well-behaved gloomy naughty clumsy complex gentle crazy rude secretive anxious deceitful violent sane repulsive cheerful reluctant wise honest calm open attractive simple sorrowful intelligent miserly

2. Antonyms of adjectives are often made with the prefixes ***un-***, ***in-***, ***dis-*** and ***im-*** (with words beginning with ***m*** or ***p***, e.g. *im**p**ossible*). Others are made by changing the suffix ***-ful*** to ***–less***, e.g. *care**ful*** ⟶ *care**less***.

Can you add prefixes or change the suffixes to make the opposites of these adjectives?

a	pleasant	______	**b**	capable	______
c	attentive	______	**d**	satisfactory	______
e	harmful	______	**f**	emotional	______
g	perfect	______	**h**	comfortable	______
i	fearful	______	**j**	obedient	______
k	respectful	______	**l**	sensitive	______
m	loyal	______	**n**	patient	______

Read and learn

Reading poetry is a good way to learn new, creative ways of expressing your ideas. Poems often contain words used in unusual ways, and metaphors and similes to express ideas.

Read the 'feelings' poem below and then answer the questions which follow.

I'm grumpy because I'm lumpy by Bill Condon

I'm mean and I'm bad—
Forgive me, Dad.
I'm grim and I'm glum—
I'm sorry, Mum.
I'm in a porcupine mood
And I'm bound to be rude ...
So please warn Janice and Stephen and Joel,
Any funny remarks and heads will roll!
I'll jump up and down
And I'll rant and I'll roar
If they giggle and cackle
And start to guffaw.

I'll be Dracula and Wolf Man
Rolled into one—
And you'll almost forget
I'm your lovable son!

On my nose there's a pimple as big as a house
Just mention it once and it's war.
With a bit of luck it'll go in a month,
Until then,
Please slide food under my door.

From *Don't throw rocks at Chicken Pox*, Angus & Robertson, 1993.

1. Why is the boy in the poem grumpy?
2. Where is he?
3. Why is the boy compared to a porcupine?
4. What else is he compared to? Why?
5. What does 'bound to be rude' mean?
   a have to be rude **b** want to be rude **c** certain to be rude
6. What does the poet mean by 'heads will roll'?
7. Which word means ...
   a 'shout like a mad person'?
   b 'laugh loudly'?
   c 'very sad'?
8. **a** What **simile** is used to describe the pimple?
   b What **metaphor** is used to describe what will happen if anyone mentions it?
9. Do you ever feel a little like the boy in the poem? Use a **simile** or **metaphor** to describe how you feel.

Reminder
A metaphor directly compares one thing to another, e.g. ***I'm a tiger** when I'm angry*.
A simile also compares two things, but uses *like...* or *as... as*, e.g. *I'm like a tiger when I'm angry*.

Dictionary search

Use your dictionary to find the nouns related to these adjectives.

1. patient ______________________
2. sincere ______________________
3. perfect ______________________
4. content ______________________
5. generous ______________________
6. loyal ______________________
7. enthusiastic ______________________
8. humble ______________________
9. sane ______________________
10. wise ______________________
11. simple ______________________
12. anxious ______________________

Puzzle

How many words from the unit can you find? Look for words from the **Topic spelling list** and **Killer words** as well as the **Looking at …** section.

R	A	P	O	S	S	E	S	S	I	V	E	P	L	E	A	S	A	N	T
A	C	O	M	F	O	R	T	A	B	L	E	R	C	B	C	U	J	G	H
T	O	U	B	G	Z	N	P	N	J	O	Q	O	S	C	A	R	E	D	O
H	M	I	R	O	A	Q	K	N	L	R	M	U	M	D	V	P	L	H	U
E	P	C	B	I	R	U	A	O	D	N	P	D	K	I	G	R	J	K	G
R	E	P	S	W	O	A	T	Y	J	E	A	L	O	U	S	I	D	I	H
H	T	Q	Q	Y	V	U	B	E	M	B	A	R	R	A	S	S	E	D	T
X	I	T	K	P	F	G	S	D	A	S	F	I	E	N	I	E	M	N	W
R	T	I	N	Q	U	I	S	I	T	I	V	E	W	X	N	D	D	V	Y
D	I	S	A	P	P	O	I	N	T	E	D	Y	W	I	C	O	L	F	L
E	V	D	W	O	R	R	I	E	D	U	H	E	U	O	E	X	N	S	G
S	E	C	R	E	T	I	V	E	F	S	T	V	C	U	R	H	X	J	D
L	R	O	X	D	E	T	E	R	M	I	N	E	D	S	E	U	M	Z	T

Your turn to write

Choose one of the following tasks.

1. Write a poem about one kind of feeling. Use the feeling as the title for your poem and then write about the experience(s) which make you feel that way. You could write, for example, about happiness, anger, joy, contentment, jealousy, freedom, loneliness, sadness or hatred.

OR

2. Follow this simple pattern to write a poem about everyday things and how they make you feel:
   Playing with my baby brother. Contented.
   Facing the weekly spelling test. Anxious.
   Lying by the pool in the warm sunshine. Calm.
   Coming first in the cross country race. Proud.
   Reading my favourite books in bed at night. Perfectly happy.

   Begin by brainstorming some ideas. Try to use vivid images.

☞ Answers on page 150

9 Music and dance

Quick fun

We often use the word ***masterpiece*** to describe a production of great skill and beauty in music, dance or other creative arts.

There are lots and lots of little words in MASTERPIECE because of all the vowels. How many can you find? (I found 55.) Give yourself a time limit of 2 minutes or you'll be looking forever!

Use this space to write out your topic words the first time. Use your own paper for extra practice.

Topic spelling list

tune	instrument
melody	choir
classical	chorus
concert	orchestra
musician	audience
musical	rehearse
performance	ballet
symphony	theatre
opera	entertainment
popular	choreographer
conductor	extravaganza

Top performance strategy

Think of related words when spelling. It is easier to get *musician* correct if you remember *music* and *musical*. Can you see any other words in the list that might be related?

Learn the words from the **Topic spelling list** using all the strategies you have learnt so far.

Rewrite here those you had most trouble with.

Fill in the gaps

Fill in the gaps with words from the **Topic spelling list**. Add or change endings where needed.

1. The ____________ waited patiently for the ____________ to arrive and for the ____________ to strike up their ____________. Only then could the curtains open.
2. Our Year 6 singing group will be in the Combined Schools ____________ at the Gala ____________. We'll be accompanied by the Sydney ____________ Orchestra!
3. My Mum and Dad love ____________, but I can't stand it. My brother, Jay, says the singers sound like they're being strangled. Dad says his music has no ____________ at all—just noise!
4. My cousin and I both do ____________, but she does classical and I do modern and jazz.
5. My friend Sasha wants to be a ____________ when she grows up—either a violinist or a pianist. She's just crazy about ____________ music, especially Beethoven and Mozart.
6. My auntie Katy belongs to the local ____________ society. She would love to play a lead role, but so far she has only sung in the ____________.
7. Everyone thought our ____________ at the end of year concert was fantastic. Everyone in the ____________ stood up and cheered—a standing ovation!
8. The word 'pop' comes from '____________'. It includes rock and roll, disco and hip hop.
9. My parents reckon pop music just recycles ____________ from their day, but I don't believe it.
10. The dancers ____________ their steps for hours before the ____________ was happy with them.
11. Everyone was looking forward to the wonderful ____________ being organised to celebrate the city's 100th birthday.

Killer words

Study these tricky words and tips and then write them without looking back.

piano	Say *PI-ANO*, not *PI-YANO*.	____________
mirror	The ***r*** is reflected (as in a mi**rr**or), so double it.	____________
public	No ***k*** at the end. Think of *publi**c**ation* and *publi**c**ity*.	____________
exhausted	Use a spelling pronunciation to remember the ***h***.	____________
queue	Use a spelling pronunciation: *KYEW-EE-EW-EE*.	____________
rhythm	Remember: ***r**hythm **h**elps **y**our **t**wo **h**ips **m**ove*.	____________

Write three sentences using the **Killer words**—two words in each.

____

____

____

Looking at … *le*, *al* and *el* words

Many English words end with a sound like ***eh + l*** (the *schwa*). Mostly this sound is spelt ***al***, ***le*** and ***el*** (and occasionally ***ol***, e.g. *car**ol***, *symb**ol***). You can sometimes guess the right ending using the following guidelines:

- ***al*** is often an adjectival ending, e.g. *music**al***
- ***le*** is often a noun ending, e.g. *troub**le***
- ***el*** often occurs after ***n***, ***r***, ***s***, ***w***, ***v*** and soft ***c*** and ***g***.

Always check the dictionary if in doubt.

1 Learn the words below and then choose from the lists to complete the puzzle below.

al		*le*		*el*
capital	comical	spectacle	sample	tunnel
theatrical	physical	principle	dazzle	barrel
principal	general	article	juggle	marvel
material	interval	miracle	supple	cancel
serial	punctual	circle	stumble	model
visual	individual	title	struggle	angel

2 Which word from the list fits these cryptic clues? Use your dictionary if in doubt.

a Main person (school, dance group). ______________________

b Rule or policy. ______________________

c How a dancer's body must be. ______________________

d Might be a city, a letter or just rather good. ______________________

e Performers can't be late, they must be … ______________________

f Something good for the eyes (in two ways). ______________________

g The show can't go on. We must … ______________________

h Time for a short break. ______________________

i If a performance is this good, it might … ______________________

j The name of the show. ______________________

3 Write four short sentences, combining one word from the **Topic spelling list** and one word from the **Looking at …** section above in each sentence, e.g. *The conductor **stumbled** as he took the platform.* Use your own paper.

Proofreading

Oh dear! There are lots of mistakes in this draft advertisement. Can you correct them before the advertisement gets printed?

Musicel event of the year

The West in Performanse

Civic Thetre, July 20

Featuring: Three student orkestras · 100-strong combined schools kwir · Classical, modern and jazz ballay · Musishans and dancers from over forty schools · Poppular and classical musick — even operah! · Rock and jazz bands · Individuel and group performences

Guest chorographer: Jack Bellini   Guest conducter: Rose Younan

Don't miss this very special consert.
Mark the date on your calender now!
Tickets availible to the publick from June 20
Avoid the queque on the night and get front row seats now.
Special prizes for lucky audence members

Vocabulary power

Even if you don't know the exact meanings of **Latin and Greek word roots**, you can often work out a rough meaning from thinking about words you know. This will help you work out new words you meet.

1 Can you work out the meanings of these common word roots by looking at the words in which they appear? Your answer does not have to be exactly right—just a rough idea.

- **a** telephone, microphone, symphony, phonograph — ***phon*** means ________
- **b** audience, audible, audiotape, audition — ***audio*** means ________
- **c** video, revise, television, evidence — ***video/vis*** means ________
- **d** finish, finalise, final, finale, infinity — ***fin*** means ________
- **e** liberate, liberty, liberal — ***liber*** means ________
- **f** local, locality, location, locate — ***locus*** means ________
- **g** memory, remember, memento — ***memor*** means ________
- **h** portable, export, import, important, support — ***port*** means ________
- **i** magnificent, magnify, main — ***magnus*** means ________
- **j** conduct, introduce, educate, abduct, product — ***duc*** means ________

2 Now use your answers from 1 above to guess the meanings of the words in **bold**. Write one or two words only and then check your dictionary to see if you were right.

- **a** The teacher taught the children to read using **phonics**. ________
- **b** She worked as an **audiologist** at the district hospital. ________
- **c** The disease affected the **auditory** nerves. ________
- **d** We were **confined** to the classroom for one hour. ________

e His **portfolio** contained all his work for the past year. ____________________

f My great-grandfather wrote his **memoirs** of his war years. ____________________

g The man was **deported** when he could not produce his passport. ____________________

h The old man was an industry **magnate** and so had lots of money. ____________________

Read and learn

Read the text below about the origins of music, taking particular notice of the words in **bold**.

How did music begin?

I'm sure you have walked through a forest or along a beach and listened to the sounds of nature, or listened to the rain on the roof or a bird singing. Well, the **theory** is that this is how music began—with humans taking notice of the sounds in their surroundings and then imitating them. Of course we'll never really know.

Another kind of music came with the development of dance. Humans needed some sort of **accompaniment** for their dancing. So they used their hands, fingers and feet with various **implements** from their environment: stones, skins, and sticks. One of the first instruments was certainly the drum, and then other kinds of percussion instruments. Often the music of these primitive peoples had religious **significance**; it was not purely for pleasure.

There is a Greek legend that the god, Pan, invented the first musical instrument, but it is pure **fancy**. It goes like this: one day, Pan sighed through the reeds on a river bank and heard his breath produce a **mournful wail**. He is said to have broken the reeds off in unequal lengths and bound them together to produce the first instrument: the shepherd's pipe, or as we usually call them—panpipes—after their inventor!

Panpipes were certainly some of the earliest wind instruments, as were whistles (primitive flutes) made of bone, wood and clay. Animal horns were, however, probably the first wind instruments—**crude** but effective. (Modern brass instruments developed from these: trumpets, cornets, tubas, and so on.) When man began to use reeds he was able to produce natural tones of much greater **delicacy**.

Strings were the last kind of musical instrument developed. First there were simple harps and **lyres**, and then other instruments played with a bow: **lutes** and violins, for example. Of course, now we have many, many kinds of instruments, but all belong to the four basic groups: percussion, wind, brass and strings.

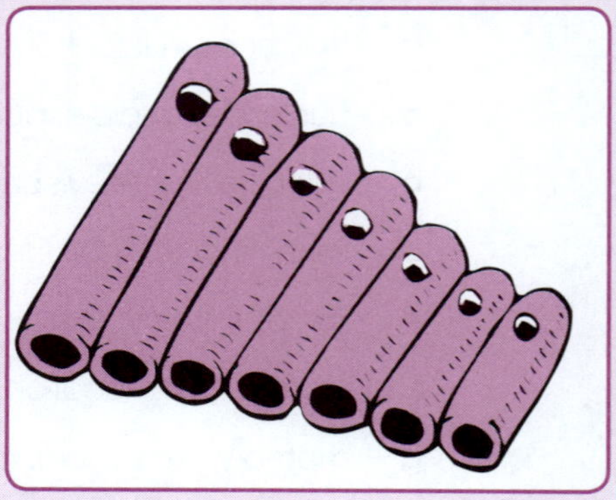

1 Choose the answers that are closest in meaning to the words a–k as used in the text.

a	theory	i	facts	ii	unproved idea	iii	imagination
b	accompaniment	i	something to go with	ii	something comical	iii	something to do
c	implements	i	musical instruments	ii	tools	iii	possessions
d	significance	i	meaning	ii	understanding	iii	ritual
e	fancy	i	liking	ii	imagination	iii	misunderstanding
f	mournful	i	sad	ii	sudden	iii	loud
g	wail	i	sigh	ii	cry	iii	pain
h	crude	i	basic	ii	rude	iii	clever

i delicacy — i allowing fine differences of sound — ii allowing softer sounds

j lyres — i stringed instruments — ii trumpet-like instruments

k lutes — i percussion instruments — ii stringed instruments

2 Look up any words you did not know in your dictionary.

Do you know this word?

The adjective ***cacophony*** is a terrific word to describe a harsh, unpleasant (usually loud) sound. Do you recognise the ***phon*** root?

*Oh no! Tom's practising his violin. What a **cacophony**!*

Puzzle

1 Can you find four words from the **Topic spelling list** in the jumbled letters?

C O N T H E O R T R A C E R T I R C H E S I E N C E A T R E A U D C H O

a ______________________ b ______________________

c ______________________ d ______________________

2 Now can you unscramble these musical instruments and put them in their correct instrument group? (They weren't all in the unit, but I'm sure you know them all.) There are six in each group.

TUFLE	BATU	GLUBE	PETTRUM	TENARCLI	EOOB	PHOAXONES	SABSOON
ONGG	JABNO	EXOPHONLY	BALCYMS	GELTRAIN	NAPIO	NATCASTES	
TULE	COOLPIC	TENROC	INLIOV	GONSOB	ONEROTMB	EKULEEL	PHAR

Wind instruments	Brass instruments	Stringed instruments	Percussion

Your turn to write

Imagine the scene. You go to see an orchestral concert. Tell us about the first ten minutes. Describe:

- waiting for the concert to start
- who you can see
- how the audience reacts
- how it starts
- what it sounds like
- how you feel

Remember to revise and edit before writing out your final draft.

☞ Answers on pages 150–151

10 Measuring up

Quick fun

These two-dimensional and three-dimensional geometric shapes are missing their consonants. What are they?

1. __ __ U __ __ E
2. __ __ IA __ __ __ E
3. __ E __ __ A __ __ __ E
4. __ I __ __ __ E
5. O __ __ A __ O __
6. __ O __ E
7. __ U __ E
8. __ __ __ I __ __ E __
9. __ __ __ E __ E
10. __ __ __ A __ I __

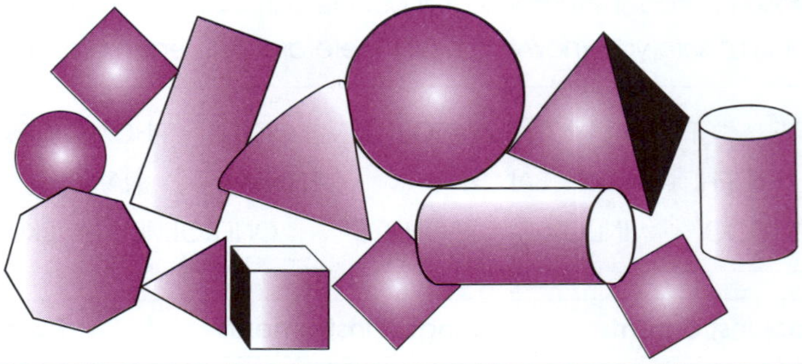

Use this space to write out your topic words the first time. Use your own paper for extra practice.

Topic spelling list

length	measure
weight	diameter
height	equal
depth	scale
width	perimeter
accurate	diagonal
dimension	hexagonal
calculate	circumference
distance	perpendicular
prism	irregular
volume	symmetrical

Space-saving strategy

Learn words together to save space in your memory, e.g. *weight* and *height*. Which other words from the list could you group together to learn?

Learn the words from the **Topic spelling list,** grouping words in a way that helps you remember any word parts.

Rewrite here those you had most trouble with.

Fill in the gaps

Fill in the gaps with words from the **Topic spelling list**. Change the word endings where necessary.

1. We have been doing a lot of work lately estimating ____________________. We had to guess how far different buildings were from our school.
2. Last week in our maths lesson, we measured the ____________________ of the car wheel and then ____________________ how many revolutions it would take to travel one kilometre.
3. This morning, we all set out to measure the ____________________ of the school. Some of us stepped it out, others used a trundle wheel and others used string. Along the way, we found out that the school was not at all ____________________. One side was much longer than the other.
4. For homework we had to work out the ____________________ of a space at home. I measured my bedroom. I found it easy to measure the ____________________ and ____________________, but I had to climb up on the cupboard to measure the ____________________.
5. Kira measured her amazing ____________________ swimming pool. It was 4x4x4x4x4x4 metres! The ____________________ was 1.5 metres at one end and 2 metres at the other.
6. In class today, we looked at word roots and prefixes. The words '____________________' and '____________________' both begin with the prefix ***dia*** meaning 'passing through'.
7. The word '____________________' means the amount of space taken up by a liquid or gas, but it also means how loud or soft a sound is.
8. Mr Anton asked us to guess the ____________________ of various objects in the classroom and then we weighed them to check how ____________________ our guesses were. Some objects looked much heavier than others, but were actually of ____________________ weight.
9. Tomorrow we are going to do some ____________________ of the classroom and then try to draw a map of it to ____________________.
10. We are also learning about rectangular, triangular and other kinds of ____________________, and collecting examples from home and school.

Killer words

Study these tricky words and tips and then write them without looking back.

exactly	Say this word correctly and you won't make a mistake.	____________________
double	Use a spelling pronunciation and learn with *trouble*.	____________________
enough	Learn with *tough* and *rough*.	____________________
surface	You ***surf*** on the ***surf***ace of the waves.	____________________
parallel	Think of two parallel bars to get the double ***l***.	____________________
angle	*Angle* or *angel*? An *angel* uses *gel* in her hair.	____________________

Use the **Killer words** in sentences to describe some things in your bedroom, e.g. a cupboard, a jewellery box, etc. Use your own paper.

Looking at … *ate* words

Many words end in ***ate***. In some words, mostly verbs, you can hear the long ***a*** sound clearly, e.g. *calcul**a**te*. But in other words, mostly adjectives, you hear the *schwa* sound, e.g. *accur**a**te*.
Some words have two pronunciations, e.g. *separ**a**te* with a long ***a*** sound is the verb and *separ**a**te* with a *schwa* sound is the adjective.

1 Learn the words below and then write them out in alphabetical order. Use your own paper.

ate **(long vowel sound)**			***ate*** **(*schwa* sound)**		
complicate	separate	eradicate	accurate	considerate	fortunate
rotate	candidate	create	approximate	appropriate	immediate
educate	isolate	template	adequate	legitimate	deliberate
debate	anticipate	estimate	delicate	separate	certificate
vacate	investigate		private	estimate	

2 Which ***ate*** words from the lists above do you sometimes use in mathematics, for example in measuring or in geometry? ____________________

____

3 Which ***ate*** words are jumbled up here? (Their synonyms are in brackets.)

a TANTORFUE (lucky) __________ b ATPETMLE (model) __________

c ATEPRSEA (divide) __________ d CADREAITE (get rid of) __________

e TONERCATESID (kind) __________ f PAPPORTERIA (suitable) __________

g BREDTALIEE (intentional) __________ h TEACRE (make) __________

i MATGELITIE (lawful) __________ j ELEDCITA (fine) __________

Looking at … measurement words

Measurement words are not difficult, but they all look similar and this can lead to spelling mistakes.

1 Make sure you know all the measurement words below. Then cover them up and write them out next to the matching abbreviation. Check your own spelling.

metre	milligram
millilitre	kilometre
millimetre	kilogram
gram	litre
centimetre	tonne

cm __________ km __________

kg __________ t __________

ml __________ mg __________

m __________ l __________

g __________ mm __________

2 Write true answers to these questions using full forms (not abbreviations).

a How tall are you? __________

b How much do you weigh? __________

c How much milk does your family buy each week (on average)? __________

d How much milk or water do you drink each day (on average)? __________

e Approximately how far is it to the shops nearest your house? __________

f How much do you think a car would weigh? __________

Proofreading

Can you correct these students' brief reports of their group maths experiments?

- Our group used three dimensonal objects to build a tower two meters high.
- We made a large sircle in the playground using only two people, a rope and chalk. We then measurd the diametre and the sircumferense.
- We surveyed 20 students to find out how far they though the school was from the Post Office: about one kilametre, more or less. We then meashured it exackly using a trundle wheel, and found only one student got the anser correct.
- Our group planned a fun run in the streets of our suberb and drew a map of the route to skale. Kindergarten to Year 3 will run 500 mitres and Years 4–6 will do dubble that distence.
- We calcated approximatly how long the bus trip would take for our excursion, and we were right.
- We each estimatted the dimentions of varous objects, and then mesured them. Each of us got an ekwal number correct. We were serprised at how acurate our gesses were.
- We experimented with paper planes to find the best modle. We varied the waight, lenthgth and width of the paper, and the angels of the folds.

Vocabulary power

There are **Latin or Greek prefixes** (sometimes both) for all numbers one to ten: ***mono*** (one), ***duo/bi*** (two), ***tri*** (three), ***quad*** (four), ***quin/pent*** (five), ***sex/hex*** (six), ***sept/hept*** (seven), ***oct*** (eight), ***nono*** (nine), ***dec*** (ten).

1 Which words with one of the prefixes above am I thinking of? You will definitely need your dictionary for some of these.

a **Three** children born at the same time. ______________________

b **Five** children born at the same time. ______________________

c **One** person or group owning everything. ______________________

d An athletics competition with **ten** events. ______________________

e Able to speak **two** languages fluently. ______________________

f A series of **three** books. ______________________

g A **four**-sided court surrounded by buildings. ______________________

h An **eight**-legged sea creature. ______________________

i To multiply by **four**. ______________________

j A sports competition with **three** events. ______________________

k A **five**-sided figure. ______________________

l A person in their **nine**ties. ______________________

Did you know?

The last four months of the year are based on Latin number prefixes. However, our calendar system is different from the ancient Roman calendar, so now the number order is not quite right.

September is now the ninth month of the year, but it used to be the seventh in the Roman calendar.

October is now the tenth. Which month do you think it used to be? What about November? Or December?

2 Now see if you can be really clever! You might need someone's help with these.

a Which word is also the name of the building which houses the United States Defence Department? ______________________

b What might a person in their eighties be called (look at **1**)? ______________________

c The word root ***pod*** means 'foot'. What do you think we call …

i ten-legged creatures like crabs? ______________________

ii eight-legged creatures like **1 h**? ______________________

Read and learn

When you meet new words in reading, try to make a rough guess at the meanings and keep reading. This will often be enough to make sense of the text. Go back to the new words when you have finished your reading and, if you need to, look them up in the dictionary.

Read the story below. Then go back and think about the words in **bold** before doing the task below.

Archimedes

Even if you have never heard of Archimedes, this picture might **ring a bell**. It **illustrates** the well-known tale of Archimedes running naked through the streets, and shouting 'Eureka!' ('I have found it!'). This great man was so excited about his most recent discovery that he forgot to put on any clothes!

Archimedes lived in the ancient Greek colony of Syracuse, Sicily, in the second century BC. He is considered by many to be one of the greatest mathematicians of all time. He was also a **physicist**, an engineer, an astronomer, a philosopher and an inventor.

While the list of his achievements is truly impressive, it is the story about running naked from the bath that most people know. The story goes that the king of Syracuse asked Archimedes if he could tell whether his royal crown contained any silver, without destroying the crown in the process.

One day as Archimedes was lowering himself into his bath, he noticed the gradual rise of the water as he got in. He realised that the water was being displaced by his body. This was the **insight** he needed to solve the king's problem. And this was when he is said to have run wildly through the streets.

Archimedes weighed the crown, dropped it in water and measured the rise in level. Then he did the same with a lump of gold of the same weight. If the crown was pure gold, the rise would have been the same. But it was not. By repeating the experiment with silver, he found the exact proportions of the two metals in the crown. His discovery led to what is now called *The Archimedes* ***Principle***.

The story about running through the town may be **exaggerated** but there is other evidence that Archimedes may have been **absent-minded**. In fact it may have cost him his life. When the city was **besieged** by enemy soldiers, he carried on with his work, so **absorbed** that he did not notice the chaos of battle around him. It is said that Archimedes pleaded with the soldier not to kill him until he had finished the mathematical task he was doing, but unfortunately **to no avail**.

A truly remarkable man.

1 Choose the answers that are closest in meaning to the words **a–j** as they are used in the text.

a	ring a bell	**i** alarm you	**ii** remind you	**iii** teach you
b	illustrates	**i** draws	**ii** throws light on	**iii** shows
c	physicist	**i** physics expert	**ii** special doctor	**iii** expert in physical fitness
d	insight	**i** idea	**ii** understanding	**iii** imagination
e	principle	**i** main point	**ii** rule to explain something	**iii** standard
f	exaggerated	**i** completely false	**ii** a lie	**iii** made more interesting than it was
g	absent-minded	**i** not present	**ii** forgetful	**iii** stupid
h	besieged	**i** surrounded in battle	**ii** bombed	**iii** threatened
i	absorbed	**i** soaked up	**ii** forgetful	**iii** totally concentrating
j	to no avail	**i** not achieving a purpose	**ii** not available	**iii** not a good idea

2 Look up any other words you don't know in your dictionary.

Puzzle

Can you complete the 'no clue' puzzle below using words from the unit?

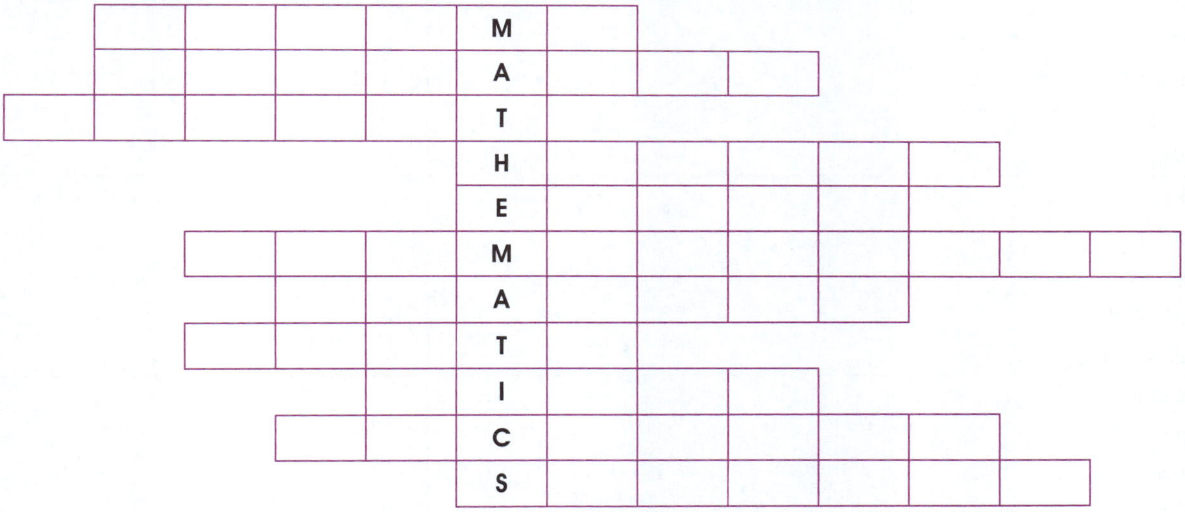

Your turn to write

Have you done any interesting mathematics work in your class involving measuring or working with geometric shapes? Write about one task or experiment you enjoyed.

Begin by saying what the purpose of the task or experiment was. Then recount what you did and what you found out.

Use these headings to structure your writing:

- Aim
- Equipment
- Method
- Result
- Conclusion.

☞ Answers on pages 151–152

Review 2

Now let's see what you remember of the words you learnt in Units 6–10. There are four tests in this review. You could do all in one session, or you could break them up and do them over a few days.

Step 1 Look at each group of words in the test to revise the spellings.
Step 2 Cover the five words up and test yourself (column 2). Try to do all five words in one go.
Step 3 Write your score out of 5 in the box. If you got any words wrong, go back and study them again.
Step 4 If possible, ask someone to test you on the words later—an hour or even a day later (column 3).

Test 1

Study	Test yourself	Test with another person
pyramid tomb secrete ancient photograph	/5	/5
palace treasure decipher pharaoh jewellery	/5	/5
religious worship nephew alphabet catastrophe	/5	/5
conquer period sphere trophy during	/5	/5
physical reign triumph eventually statue	/5	/5
intriguing style series exciting mystery	/5	/5
	Total score = out of 30	Total score = out of 30

Test 2

Study	Test yourself	Test with another person
dialogue genre hilarious thoroughly various	/5	/5
humorous author atmosphere fantasy ridiculous	/5	/5
favourite recommend though enjoyable beginning	/5	/5
enormous famous character adventurous marvellous	/5	/5
calm proud annoyed frightened anxious	/5	/5
surprised rather worried jealous sensitive	/5	/5
	Total score = out of 30	Total score = out of 30

Test 3

Study	Test yourself	Test with another person
disappointed determined competitive comfortable embarrassed	/5	/5
imaginative scared laugh thought pleasant	/5	/5
classical concert musician popular instrument	/5	/5
orchestra audience rehearse theatre mirror	/5	/5
public exhausted queue model material	/5	/5
general interval choir individual spectacle	/5	/5
	Total score = out of 30	Total score = out of 30

Which word?

1. Her ________________________ was affected by the accident. (*site, sight*)
2. They found many treasures at the archaeological ________________________. (*site, sight*)
3. ________________________ that knocking at the door? (*Who's, Whose*)
4. ________________________ jumper is this? (*who's, whose*)

Test 4

Study	Test yourself	Test with another person
volume juggle rhythm struggle cancel	/5	/5
sample length height calculate depth	/5	/5
width accurate weight distance measure	/5	/5
dimension immediate perpendicular considerate exactly	/5	/5
double enough surface parallel estimate	/5	/5
approximate symmetrical diagonal separate angle	/5	/5
	Total score = out of 30	Total score = out of 30

5 A ______________ can be a rule, but it can also be a standard of behaviour. (*principle, principal*)

6 The ______________ dancer got the greatest applause. (*principle, principal*)

7 Thank you for your help. You're a real ______________. (*angle, angel*)

8 Draw a 90 degree ______________. (*angle, angel*)

9 His face was badly ______________. (*scared, scarred*)

10 I am really ______________ of heights. (*scared, scarred*)

Good work!

☞ Answers on page 152

11 Reaching the poles

Quick fun

Can you unscramble these polar animals and birds? Some are found in the Arctic, others in the Antarctic.

1. UPENING ____________
2. SAWRUL ____________
3. LASE ____________
4. ALTBASSOS ____________
5. LETPER ____________
6. ASKU ____________
7. ANTROMROC ____________
8. RENT ____________
9. BARICOU ____________

Topic spelling list

temperature	trek
iceberg	depot
blizzard	territory
remote	explorer
glacier	expedition
terrain	extreme
feat	compass
discovered	endurance
journey	crevasse
pioneer	fatigue
route	accompany

Legendary strategy

Spelling difficult words out loud and with rhythm can really help you remember them, because you have to picture the spellings in your head as you spell them out.

Spell the words from the **Topic spelling list** out loud and then write them out. **Note:** *crevasse* is pronounced with the stress on the second syllable (to rhyme with *alas*).

Use this space to write out your topic words the first time. Use your own paper for extra practice.

Rewrite here those you had most trouble with.

Fill in the gaps

Fill in the gaps with words from the **Topic spelling list**. Add endings if needed.

1. Polar adventurers had to face ____________ weather conditions: freezing ____________ and raging ____________. Not only that, they had to conquer difficult ____________ including mountains, ____________ and crevasses.
2. There have been many great ____________ of courage and ____________ during the history of polar exploration. It is difficult to imagine the extreme discomfort and ____________ these explorers must have experienced.
3. The first Arctic explorers were the native Inuit, even though their ____________ have not been documented. These indigenous people have learnt to survive in the most ____________ region of the world.
4. There have been many attempts to find a ____________ across the top of the world: the Northwest Passage. Almost all ended in disaster but finally in 1905, Roald Amundsen was successful.
5. The first person to reach the South Pole, on 14 December 1911, was the Norwegian ____________ Roald Amundsen, beating Robert Scott by only one month.
6. After losing the race to the South Pole, Scott and his companions died on the long ____________ home. They were only seventeen kilometres from their ____________.
7. Australia is one of seven nations that have claimed Antarctic ____________.
8. It is hard to believe that Antarctica is a ____________ when there is ice and water all around.
9. Ernest Shackleton went on two ____________ to the Antarctic. Although he never reached the pole, his courage and leadership under terrible conditions are legendary.
10. Polar explorers always have to be on the lookout for ____________ in the ice. These can be 10, 20 or even 40 metres deep, and covered with thin bridges of snow.
11. Modern polar adventurers tend to use Global Positioning System (GPS) to find their way around because ____________ are affected by the magnetic pull of the poles.

Killer words

Study these tricky words and tips and then write them without looking back.

icy	Drop the **e** when changing *ice* to *icy*.	____________
island	Remember: there *is land* in *island*.	____________
diary	Don't confuse with *dairy* (for cows).	____________
successful	Chant out loud till you know it.	____________
Antarctic	To get the middle **c**, remember there is an ***arc*** at both	____________
Arctic	poles, and pronounce the words distinctly.	____________

Can you use all the **Killer words** in one sentence? I'm sure you can.

____

Looking at … soft c and sc words

Many words have a **c** for the **s** sound if it is followed by ***e***, ***i*** or ***y***, e.g. *gla**c**ier*. This is called a soft **c**. Some words have both ***s*** and ***c***, e.g. ***sc**ientist*.

1 Learn the words below, checking the meaning of any you are not sure of in your dictionary. Ask someone to test you on them when you have finished the section.

scientist	service	decide	advance	fascinating
scenery	citizen	decision	chance	excel
since	civilised	century	advice	excellent
silence	circulation	balance	notice	except
accidental	circumstance	precise	balance	exceed
cinema	incident	announce	disgrace	excessive

2 Match words from the list to the clues below.

a do very well ____________ **b** opportunity ____________

c too much ____________ **d** opposite of *retreat* ____________

e shame ____________ **f** determine ____________

g exact, accurate ____________ **h** steadiness ____________

i movie theatre ____________ **j** to state, report ____________

k go beyond ____________ **l** situation ____________

Looking at … apostrophe of possession

We use an **apostrophe** to show that a person or a thing owns or possesses another, e.g. *Peter's uncle is a scientist*. (*Peter's uncle = the uncle of Peter*)

You only have to remember **one thing** about where to put the apostrophe. You put it **immediately after** the person/thing that does the owning, e.g.

Peter's uncle = *the uncle of Peter* → the apostrophe goes after *Peter* → *Peter's*
the explorers' families = *the families of the explorers* → the apostrophe goes after *explorers* → *explorers'*
the men's goal = *the goal of the men* → the apostrophe goes after *men* → *men's*

1 Put an apostrophe where needed in these sentences.

a The scientists achievement was extraordinary. She deserves her award.
b I was allowed to look in the two scientists diaries.
c The explorers tale of his lonely Antarctic journey was very moving.
d The survivors stories of their time underground were truly shocking.
e The rescuers left the mens possessions where they found them.

2 Put an apostrophe where needed in these sentences. Don't put one if there is no owning or possessing.

a The explorers never met up again.
b The two adventurers could not agree on the best route to take.
c The scientists families were very proud of their achievements.
d The womens team reached camp before the mens team.
e The dogs stayed with their masters till the end.

Proofreading

Can you help this student revise his draft for a school project? Remember there might be words from previous units.

Antartica: Some fasinating facts

- Amazingly, Antartica is far drier than the center of Australia. The average rainfall is just 200 milimetres—less than half the rainfall of Australia and just a little more than the Sahara Dessert.
- It is the coldest and windiest place on earth. The temprature can go down to minus 90 degres Celsius. Winds of up to 320 kilametres regularly blow across the permenent icey cover.
- The continent covers an area of 15.5 sqware killometres but in winter it almost dubbles in size.
- Hundreds of scintists live at the Antractic durring the summer months, doing research into global warming, the hole in the ozone layer and the greenhouse effect.
- Its tough terain and extreem wheather conditions have tested the endurence of many couragous explorors over the past scentury. It has also taken many lives. Robert Falcon Scott's team in 1912 perished on their return journy only 20 kilometers from their food depow.
- It is difficult to say when the Antarctic was acshully discuverd. Captain Cook saw islands off the coast in 1773, but the the first man to set foot on land is thought to be John Davis, an American sealer, in 1821.
- In 1997, an Australian trio reached the South Pole unaided. It was the first Australian expadition to do so, and the fifth ever.

Vocabulary power

There are many vivid, precise adjectives you can use to write about the amazing tales of **exploration**.

1. Which of the words below could you use to describe the people (explorers), the place and the weather? Are there any you could use for more than one of these subjects? Use your dictionary if you need to.

grim	intrepid	valiant	daring
hazardous	raging	majestic	bitter
magnificent	harsh	desolate	freakish
foul	selfless	extraordinary	noble
remote	heroic	mysterious	dazzling
courageous	atrocious	inspirational	sublime
ferocious	bold	abominable	violent

People	Place	Weather

2. Make up three sentences about polar exploration, combining words about people, places and weather in each. Use your own paper.

Read and learn

Reading is the very best way to enrich your vocabulary. Remember to use the dictionary or ask someone for help if you really can't work out word meanings from the context.

Read this story of Antarctic exploration, making rough guesses at the meanings of the words in **bold** before doing the activity below.

Douglas Mawson

Douglas Mawson is one of Australia's greatest heroes and a **towering** figure in the **annals** of Antarctic exploration. On November 10 1912, Mawson left his base camp on a journey across the Antarctic with his two companions, Xavier Mertz and Belgrave Ninnis.

Mertz set the pace for the dogs as they pulled the three sledges packed high with equipment and provisions. At first, their progress was quite rapid, but soon the glacial terrain became steep and **perilous**. Ninnis fell three times into crevasses and had to be hauled out.

On December 13, nature seemed to sound a warning. There were sudden thunderous cracking sounds as ice and snow collapsed deep beneath them. The next day, catastrophe struck.

Mawson and Mertz crossed a snow bridge over a crevasse and signalled Ninnis on the rear sledge to watch out for it. When they looked back, they saw with horror that there was no sign of Ninnis or his team. Ninnis had dropped into the **abyss**, the sledge and dogs falling after him. The two survivors, shocked and sickened, **took stock of** their situation. As practically all the food had gone, they realised they would have to eat the dogs to survive.

Their trip from then on was a horror stretch. Both men were weak from hunger and exhaustion and **wretched** with pain. The skin peeled off them in strips and Mawson became snowblind. As the **rigours** of the journey increased, and the **desolate** landscape lay endlessly before them, Mertz became very ill and slowly went insane. On January 8th, he died.

Mawson now had to face a 160-kilometre trek back to base—totally alone. He **resolved** to travel eight kilometres a day. And somehow, with superhuman strength and willpower, he did—even surviving a fall into a huge crevasse himself. On February 8, after an **excruciating** thirty days, Mawson staggered into camp. He had missed his ship by a few hours, but in the end this was a blessing, as it gave him time to recover from his shocking ordeal before travelling home.

Mawson's **solitary** journey against such incredible odds has deservedly made him a **legend** of Antarctic exploration.

1 Choose the answers that are closest in meaning to the words a–l as they are used in the text.

a	towering	i tall	ii great	iii good
b	annals	i annual events	ii stories	iii historical records
c	perilous	i frightening	ii slippery	iii very dangerous
d	abyss	i great hole	ii small crack	iii cliff
e	took stock of	i examined	ii wrote about	iii complained about
f	wretched	i complaining	ii miserable	iii sick
g	rigours	i difficulties	ii length	iii weariness
h	desolate	i deserted	ii difficult	iii beautiful
i	resolved	i realised	ii determined	iii tried
j	excruciating	i very long	ii very hard	iii very painful
k	solitary	i alone	ii lonely	iii long
l	legend	i great story	ii imaginary story	iii person of great fame

2 Use your dictionary or ask someone about any other words you did not know.

Dictionary search

Look up these words in your dictionary: *frostbite, pack-ice, ice-floe, permafrost, hypothermia, chasm*.

1. Which word means something like *crevasse* and *abyss*? ____________________

   Dictionaries usually give the pronunciation of words using phonetic symbols. For example, a ' is used to show where the stress goes in unusual words like ***cre ' vasse***. The list of symbols is usually given at the front of the dictionary.

2. Look up the word *abyss*. Is the stress on the first or second syllable? ____________________

3. Look again at *chasm*. Can you work out how the **ch** is pronounced? ____________________

Puzzle

How many words from the unit can you find in the grid below?

E	N	D	U	R	A	N	C	E	A	B	B	L	I	Z	Z	A	R	D
X	E	I	S	L	A	N	D	O	X	L	N	U	K	X	A	E	Q	P
P	G	A	F	H	P	Q	E	D	M	T	E	R	R	I	T	O	R	Y
E	U	R	O	U	T	E	S	G	J	P	R	H	G	O	R	Z	O	E
D	V	Y	S	F	E	C	E	D	W	I	A	E	J	K	E	L	U	F
I	B	L	M	O	R	D	R	L	I	D	Q	S	M	I	K	N	T	E
T	E	M	P	E	R	A	T	U	R	E	T	V	S	E	K	W	E	A
I	R	T	T	R	A	F	C	W	Q	P	B	M	F	M	J	A	L	T
O	K	Z	C	S	I	K	E	Z	H	O	X	J	O	U	R	N	E	Y
N	L	N	H	J	N	R	E	M	O	T	E	G	D	Y	Z	M	Y	O
U	S	U	C	C	E	S	S	F	U	L	R	G	L	A	C	I	E	R
A	V	B	D	I	S	C	O	V	E	R	E	D	Y	I	P	A	S	C

Did you know?

There are many websites about famous explorers such as Mawson, Shackleton, Scott and Amundsen. Others show what life is like in the polar regions. The website of the Australian Government Antarctic Division is a good example.

Your turn to write

Polar explorers always kept diaries to record their experiences. Imagine you are on a polar expedition. Write a diary entry for one day, using the information and words from the unit—and lots of imagination. You might also want to do some of your own research.

☞Answers on pages 152–153

12 Health, sport, fitness

Quick fun

Which six sporting activities are hidden in the letters below?
Write them in the box below.

SOCRIBAGYSWATHCCCSKMNIMICSETERKETLETASBALLMINGTICS

Topic spelling list

healthy
diet
energy
muscle
limb
exercise
physical
activity
stretch
competition
champion
frequent
regular
injury
leisure
stamina
sugar
vitamin
agility
protein
carbohydrates
tournament

Healthy hint

Remember: for words ending in a consonant + ***y***, change the ***y*** to ***i*** before adding an ending, e.g. *activity* → *activit**ies***, *healthy* → *health**ier***.

DON'T change the ***y*** when adding ***ing***, e.g. *carry* → *carry**ing***.

Learn the words from the **Topic spelling list** using any useful strategies. Then cover them up, a few at a time, and write them out.

Use this space to write out your topic words the first time. Use your own paper for extra practice.

Rewrite here those you had most trouble with.

Fill in the gaps

Fill in the gaps with words from the **Topic spelling list**. Add or change endings if necessary.

1. If you want to be fitter and ____________________, you need to ____________________ ____________________. You should also have a good ____________________.
2. To keep in good ____________________ shape, you need to use all your muscles. If you do this, you shouldn't have too many ____________________ problems when playing sport.
3. Our gym ____________________ is held at the local ____________________ centre. The best gymnasts have great strength and ____________________.
4. When my little brother was born, everyone said he would be a high-jumper or a tennis player because he had such long, long ____________________.
5. We all need to consume some ____________________ to give us the ____________________ to get through the day.
6. We did some ____________________ exercises before we set off on our mountain bushwalk, so that our leg ____________________ would not be sore the next day.
7. Foods such as potatoes, pasta, rice and bread are high in ____________________, whereas meat is high in ____________________.
8. Dad takes lots of ____________________ tablets each day, because he can't eat certain foods.
9. To be a cross-country ____________________, you need good ____________________ to be still running hard at the end.
10. At our school, we do outdoor ____________________ quite ____________________. We even have lessons outdoors.

Killer words

Study the tricky words and tips and then write them without looking back.

variety	Say the syllables *VA-RI-ET-Y* to get the vowels.	____________________
necessary	Remember: *one **c**ollar and two **s**ocks in ne**c**e**ss**ary.*	____________________
straight	Just chant it or write it out till you know it!	____________________
field	***i*** before **e** except after **c** (for long **e** sound).	____________________
practise	*Practise* is a verb, e.g. *I **practise** the piano every day.*	____________________
practice	*Practice* is a noun, e.g. *I do piano **practice** every day.*	____________________

Make up three short sentences with two **Killer words** in each.

____

____

____

Looking at … horror homophones

Here is your chance to get these tricky **homophones** sorted out, so you'll know them forever!

1. Look at the words and meanings below, and read the tips.

we're = we are	**where** = question about place	**wear** = put on (e.g. clothes)
you're = you are	**your** = belonging to you	**yore** = long ago times (unusual)
they're = they are	**their** = belonging to them (their house)	**there** = a place
who's = who is or who has	**whose** = question about belonging	
here = a place	**hear** = listen	
it's = it is or it has	**its** = belonging to it (e.g. *The dog chased **its** tail.*)	

Tip 1: Remember the place words—*here, there* and *where*—all have *here* inside them.

Tip 2: ONLY use the contractions (e.g. *we're, they're, who's*) if the word can be replaced with the full form, e.g.

*Tell them **we're** late.*	means	*Tell them **we are** late.*	(Correct!)
***We're** are you?*	means	***We are** are you?*	(This doesn't make sense: change it to ***Where** are you?*)
***It's** pouring with rain*	means	***It is** pouring with rain.*	(Correct!)
*I saw **it's** face.*	means	*I saw **it is** face.*	(This doesn't make sense: change it to *I saw **its** face.*)

2. Complete these sentences with the correct homophones from the box. There may be more than one possibility.

a You need to exercise ____________________ muscles each day.

b The new leisure centre opened ____________________ doors for the first time today.

c ____________________ trackpants are these? They weren't ____________________ this morning.

d I asked you to ____________________ shorts today.

e The children followed ____________________ fitness program for ten days.

f Do you know if ____________________ all right to use the exercise machines?

g ____________________ eating only good food for snacks now.

h So ____________________ enrolling for the swimming lessons?

i I had to ask someone ____________________ the gymnasium was.

j If ____________________ interested in getting fit, sign up for classes now.

Word scramble

Which words from the **Topic spelling list** and **Killer words** are scrambled below?

1. MASTAIN ____________________
2. HATYHEL ____________________
3. SCALIPHY ____________________
4. CHESTRT ____________________
5. IRAVYET ____________________
6. EELISUR ____________________
7. PINAMCHO ____________________
8. ICATTIVY ____________________

Proofreading

Can you check these students' sentences before they go on a poster about health, sport and fitness? Watch out for those horror homophones!

Nina: I like comppeting in swimming races. When I do well, I feel prowd and full of ennergy.

Susie: Dansing keeps me fit and helthy. If I don't do reguler excercise, I feel yucky.

Len: My favourit activitys are riding my bike and playing socer. There fun.

Suri: I do gimnastics. Its a lot of fun. They're is a lot of vairety and lots of competions.

Thea: I play netball. I don't reelly do it for pysical fitness—I do it because it's fun.

Matt: I play soccer. Before each game we strech our mussels so that we won't get injurys.

Leo: I want to be a champien tennis player, so I don't have much lesiure time. I do lots of practise.

Xavier: I do athleticks. I like running long distanse races best, but I want to improve my staminar.

Anna: I have to eat a balansed dyet because I do many sports. Proteen and carbohidrates are neccesary for me to do well, but so is suger.

Karl: I don't care whose winning when I race. I just love competing.

Vocabulary power

An **idiom** is a group of words that does not mean exactly what it says. For example, I might say *The team ran out of steam*. However, I don't mean *The team did not have any water vapour left*. I mean *They had no energy left to win*.

1. The idioms below could all be used about individuals or teams playing **sport**. Can you match them to their meanings?

Idiom	Meaning
a drag your feet	improve a great deal
b lose ground	win very easily
c make/gain ground	lose the advantage in a match or competition
d hit your stride	make progress in a match or competition
e go ahead in leaps and bounds	never give up, even though it looks like you will lose
f be home and dry (or hosed)	give up and stop trying to win
g throw in the towel	come last in a competition
h lose heart	have no chance of winning at all
i fight a losing battle	be much better than the other team or individual
j win hands down	start to do something confidently, after not being so confident
k take the wooden spoon	safely be the winner (even though the competition is not over)
l run rings around someone	go very slowly
m fight to the bitter end	start to feel discouraged because you are not winning

2. Can you think of another sporting idiom or expression—about the game, the referee, the competitors or the spectators? ______________________________

3. Use two or three of the idioms above in true sentences about your own sports activities (on your own paper.)

Read and learn

When you read, take a moment to look at how the writer has expressed ideas. This will help you with your own writing.

Read the text below and do the activities.

1 The greatest sporting event in the world is surely the Olympic Games. The Olympics attract millions of television viewers around the globe as the world's best athletes strive to run faster, jump higher, or throw further than their rivals. Track and field events probably have the widest appeal of all the Olympic events.

2 What is it about track and field athletics that appeals to so many sports lovers? Is it the blinding speed of the 100 metres sprint: the contest to decide who is the world's fastest? Is it the courageous endurance displayed by marathon runners as they push themselves through the pain barrier and complete the longest and most gruelling track event of the Games?

3 Some fans are thrilled by the magnificent heights attained by high jumpers and pole vaulters as they gracefully soar up and over the bar. Others are eager to see just how far the long and triple jumpers can propel their agile bodies through the air.

4 There is something special about watching human beings competing against each other. Like the excitement of a photo finish as competitors cross the line within split seconds of each other, straining to gain every extra centimetre.

5 Spectators often stand and cheer as the final lone competitor in a distance event struggles along to the finish line, minutes after other competitors have finished. There is always a place in our hearts for the 'underdog' in track and field events, because courage and persistence are qualities we admire as much as speed and strength.

6 What is it about track and field that you enjoy? Are you one of the millions who watch the Olympic Games on television? Do you love running, jumping or throwing? Do you dream of running faster or jumping higher than anyone has done before? Do you strive to improve on your personal best?

From *Track and Field Athletics* by Garry Chapman, Macmillan Education Australia, 1996.

1 Each of the words below could be used in the text, but in each case, the writer has used more interesting words. Go back to the paragraphs given and find the better words used. A thesaurus might help you.

a opponents (paragraph 1) ________________

b interest (paragraph 1) ________________

c try (paragraph 1) ________________

d exhausting (paragraph 2) ________________

e great (paragraph 2) ________________

f rise (paragraph 3) ________________

g interested (paragraph 3) ________________

h push (paragraph 3) ________________

i athletic (paragraph 3) ________________

j reached (paragraph 3) ________________

k trying hard (paragraph 4) ________________

l single (paragraph 5) ________________

2 Do you know what these expressions mean? Use your dictionary or ask someone if you don't know.

a pain barrier (paragraph 2)

b split second (paragraph 4)

c underdog (paragraph 5)

d personal best (paragraph 6)

Choose two of these expressions to use in true sentences of your own.

____

____

Puzzle

Across

4. A tricky question word with *hose* inside it. (5)
5. __________ makes perfect. (8)
7. This could be a kind of seafood. No, wrong spelling! (6)
8. Relating to the body. (8)
11. Often. (8)
14. Contains the word *heal*. (7)
16. Eat lean meat and fish to get this. (7)
18. Belonging to them. (5)
19. Harm to the body. (6)
20. Anagram of *tide* (the letters are scrambled). (4)

Down

1. Do you like pasta? If so, you'll be getting lots of these in your diet. (13)
2. We have four of these, but some animals have more. (5)
3. Water is an absolutely __________ part of your diet. (9)
6. Contest, rivalry. (11)
9. Not crooked. (8)
10. Time to relax. (7)
12. This could be physical or mental. (8)
13. This is important to do before doing sport. (6)
15. Strength and power to keep going. (7)
17. Range, diversity. (7)

Your turn to write

Make a poster to encourage young children to keep fit and healthy. You might give them some tips about exercise or diet, but you could also tell them about how **you** keep fit and why.

Be creative and include pictures if you wish. Remember to check your writing before you prepare your final copy.

☞ Answers on pages 153–154

13 Experimenting with science

Quick fun

Data means information. Can you change one letter each time to make DATA into something we eat? (**Hint**: it's full of carbohydrates.) Then try changing TEST into something used to change solids to liquids, or liquids to gases.

1 DATA

_ _ _ _

_ _ _ _ (speed)

_ _ _ _

_ _ _ _

2 TEST

_ _ _ _ (very good)

_ _ _ _

_ _ _ _

Use this space to write out your topic words the first time. Use your own paper for extra practice.

Topic spelling list

data	explain
prove	explanation
disprove	evaluate
procedure	materials
survey	conclusion
collect	evaporate
mixture	liquid
observe	dissolve
observation	hypothesis
investigate	theory
evidence	apparatus

Scientific strategy

Pronouncing words correctly helps you spell correctly. Say the last two consonants of *colle**ct*** distinctly and you won't forget the **c**. This will help you write related words, where it is harder to hear the separate consonants, e.g. *colle**ct**s, colle**ct**ion.*

Say all the words from the **Topic spelling list** out loud and then write them out to learn them.

Rewrite here those you had most trouble with.

Fill in the gaps

Fill in the gaps with words from the **Topic spelling list**. Change endings where necessary.

1. You have to carefully follow the ____________________ when setting up science experiments.
2. Scientists usually begin an experiment with a ____________________: a prediction about what will happen and why.
3. Scientists are rather like detectives when they ____________________ a crime. They look for ____________________ to ____________________ or ____________________ their ____________________ or hypothesis.
4. Chemical ____________________ can be dangerous, so they must be handled with care.
5. We ____________________ everyone in our school about their opinions. We had lots of ____________________ to sort through before we could work out the ____________________.
6. In Science Club, we ____________________ different kinds of insects and ____________________ them over five days.
7. I think science is fascinating because it ____________________ the way our world works.
8. We did some interesting experiments about the ____________________ of water to help us understand the weather system.
9. We normally think of water as ____________________, but of course it has two other forms: ice and water vapour.
10. For our Science Club, we bring in all kinds of ____________________ from home to use in our experiments. Sometimes we use special scientific ____________________ (pieces of equipment).

Killer words

Reminder
Be especially careful with the **plural** forms of ***ct*** words, e.g. *collecks* ✗ *collects* ✓

Study these tricky words and tips and then write them without looking back.

separate	Remember ***pa*** is caught in the middle.	____________________
cause	Learn with that other tricky word: *because*.	____________________
amount	Learn with *count: count the amount.*	____________________
carefully	Nothing to do with a *car*, so put the **e** in.	____________________
task	Pronounce the letters distinctly: *T-A-S-K*.	____________________
therefore	***re*** occurs twice: *the**re**fo**re***.	____________________

Which **Killer words** are muddled up and hidden in the middle of these six words from the **Topic spelling list**?

1. LISEAUCQUID ____________________
2. MIXUNTAMOTURE ____________________
3. THESKTAORY ____________________
4. SUREETHEFORRVEY ____________________
5. DASTEEPAARTA ____________________
6. PROFULLRECAYVE ____________________

Looking at … *ct* words

You need to be especially careful with words ending in ***ct***, e.g. *colle**ct**, fa**ct**, refle**ct***. If you don't pronounce these words correctly, you might think that they end with ***ck***. You might also make mistakes when they take endings like ***s***, ***ure*** and ***ion***.

1. Learn the ***ct*** words below, taking notice of the patterns. Ask someone to test you on them when you are sure you know them all.

fact	object	suspect	perfect	friction
pact	inspect	strict	project	reflection
exact	respect	contradict	instruct	inspection
extract	reflect	predict	construct	direction
subtract	subject	verdict	conduct	structure
contact	connect	district	extinct	lecture
elect	expect	convict	distinct	fracture

2. What **verbs** from the list above match these people's jobs? There might be more than one possibility.

   a a detective ______________ **b** a teacher ______________

   c a fortune teller ______________ **d** a builder ______________

   e a lawyer ______________ **f** a philosopher ______________

   g a mathematician ______________ **h** a dentist ______________

3. Choose words from the ***ct*** list to fill the gaps. You'll have to add an ending and/or a prefix to some.

   a The dodo is an ______________ species.

   b Your ______________ were unclear and we got lost.

   c The School Captain ______________ take place this Friday.

   d Speak ______________ so I can understand you.

   e The electricity was ______________ last night.

   f The story was extremely interesting because it was completely ______________.

   g He ______________ what he said earlier.

   h The ______________ was 'not guilty'.

Proofreading

Can you correct the mistakes in this student's unit spelling test? **Warning:** there are a few tricky words from the last two units as well. Write the correct spellings in the spaces.

dissproove	______________	couse	______________	explaination	______________
theory	______________	evaporate	______________	contacts	______________
carfully	______________	amount	______________	taks	______________

fracture	________	colleck	________	objects	________
predicks	________	neccesary	________	hypothesis	________
survey	________	evaluate	________	therefore	________
sucessful	________	conclusion	________	materiels	________
mixtur	________	prosedure	________	likwid	________
seperate	________	supspect	________	inspexion	________
variety	________	field	________	discuverd	________

Vocabulary power

You need to be clear and precise when writing about **experiments**.

1 You often have to describe materials or equipment. Which words from the box could you use to describe something …

rubbery	brittle
gritty	wringing-wet
coarse	fragile
drenched	saturated
rigid	elastic
supple	granular
inflexible	unbending
pliant	

- **a** very wet? ________
- **b** breakable? ________
- **c** unbreakable? ________
- **d** very stiff? ________
- **e** very soft? ________
- **f** rough, like sand? ________

2 Sometimes you might use words that say one thing is like something else in its appearance or texture, e.g. *sandy* means 'feels like sand'. Can you work out these? (The first three are very easy.)

- **a** like stone _ _ _ _ Y
- **b** like powder _ _ _ _ _ _ Y
- **c** like flour _ _ _ _ _ Y
- **d** like breadcrumbs _ _ _ _ _ _ Y
- **e** like cake S _ _ _ _ Y
- **f** like uncooked bread D _ _ _ _ Y
- **g** like a very smooth fabric _ _ _ _ Y
- **h** like a feather bed D _ _ _ Y

3 You also need to use precise verbs to give instructions for an experiment; these are often a little different from verbs you use in everyday conversation.
Can you match the everyday verbs below to the more precise words in the box?

release place attach examine collect observe conduct produce resemble experiment with

- **a** do (experiment) ________
- **b** put ________
- **c** watch ________
- **d** try out ________
- **e** get ________
- **f** look like ________
- **g** make ________
- **h** look at ________
- **i** let go ________
- **j** stick ________

Read and learn

There are many excellent books and magazines which tell you how to do simple science experiments. Even when you understand all the words in these instructions, you need to concentrate to understand exactly what to do.

1 Some words are missing in the text below, but you should be able to follow the instructions if you read carefully. First, read the article right through, just thinking about what the missing words could be.

Easing the tension

Feeling tense? Well, so does water; but it's a different sort of **(a)** ____________________ that makes water behave the way it does.

Water has a lot of surface tension. This means the water likes to pull together at the **(b)** ____________________. It's the reason water breaks into drops when it's sprayed from a hose. It's also why it hurts when you **(c)** ____________________ into water and do a belly flop!

There are heaps of experiments you can do with surface tension. Try this simple one. All you need to do is sprinkle some ground pepper on the surface of a bowl of fresh water. Then just add a drop of detergent to the middle of a bowl and watch the **(d)** ____________________ race for the edges.

What's happening? The detergent breaks down the water's surface tension so it 'relaxes' and tries to spread out as much as possible instead of pulling inward. As the surface of the water relaxes **(e)** ____________________, the pepper is pushed out.

You could set this up as a magic trick with your friends. Ask them if they can 'scare' the pepper to the edges of the water. When they can't, all you have to do is dip your finger in, and all the pepper will run to the **(f)** ____________________. The secret is that you've previously rubbed the tip of your finger on some soap or dipped it in **(g)** ____________________.

Be sure to wash the bowl well before you try this again. If there are any **(h)** ____________________ of soap or detergent left, the water's surface tension will be broken before you begin.

This simple experiment shows us some fascinating things about surface tension. It's one of the most important **(i)** ____________________ of water, even if we don't usually notice it.

By the way, it's not only water that has surface tension. Other liquids have it too, even detergent. However, the pulling forces of other liquids may not be as **(j)** ____________________.

Adapted from *Easing the tension* by David Harris, *The Helix*, No. 66, June–July 1999. Reproduced with permission.

2 Now choose a word from the box below to write in each space **a–j** above.

outward	detergent	tension	pepper	surface	dive	traces	strong	properties	edges

3 Now that you know what to do, why don't you try out the experiment for yourself?

Puzzle

Can you complete this crossword using words from the unit?

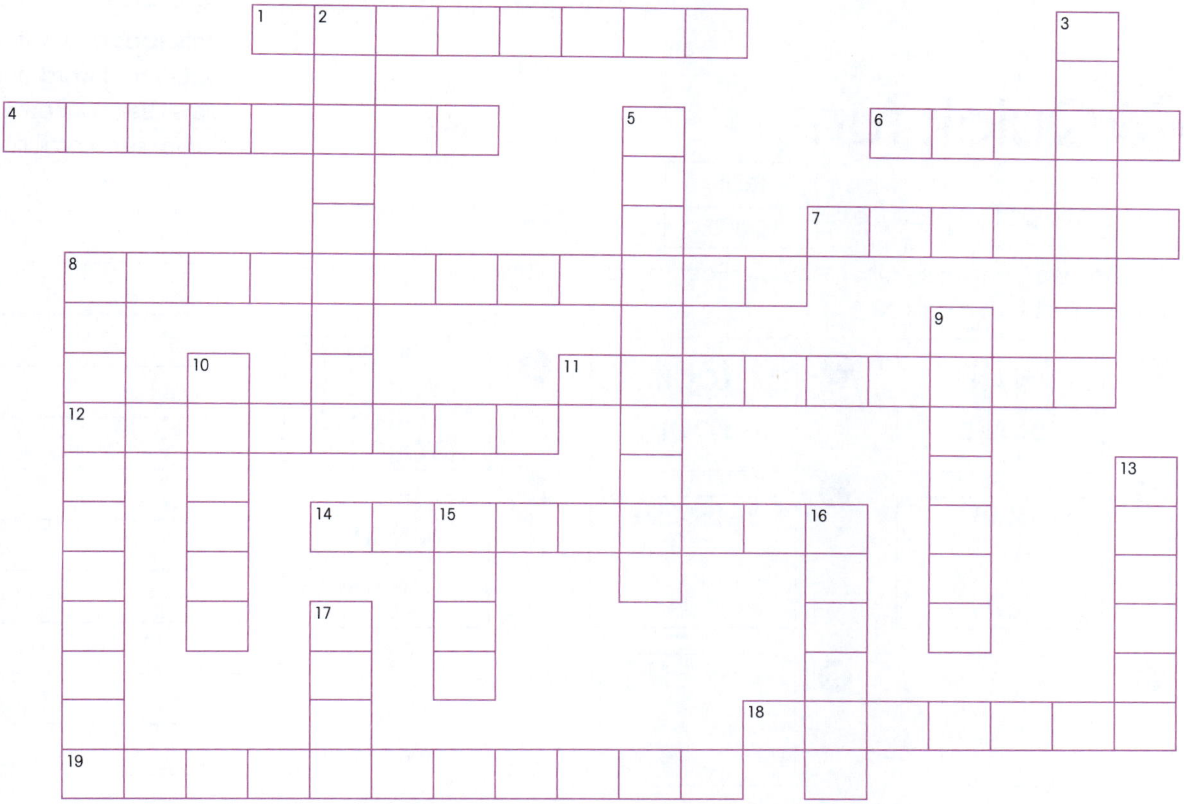

Across

1 Not together. (8)
4 Judge, assess. (8)
6 Many experiments aim to show a ___________. (5)
7 An idea (not proved). (6)
8 Directions to do something. (12)
11 So, thus. (9)
12 Proof. (8)
14 The things you need. (9)
18 Absolutely right! (7)
19 The noun from explain. (11)

Down

2 Turn into vapour. (9)
3 The opposite of *prove*. (7)
5 Prediction about what will happen and why. (10)
8 Scientists and detectives do this. (11)
9 Gather things. (7)
10 Solid, gas, ___________. (6)
13 This can be a thing or a verb meaning 'oppose'. (6)
15 A job to do. (4)
16 A research method where you ask lots of questions. (6)
17 Information, facts. (4)

Your turn to write

The pictures below show how to do a simple water experiment. If you have done the experiment, you'll know it can turn out messy if you don't do it correctly! If you haven't done the experiment, do it now based on the pictures.

BUT DO IT OVER THE SINK!

Now write a procedure for the experiment that someone else could follow.

- Give your experiment a name.
- Write a list of equipment or materials.
- Write a set of numbered steps.
- Give your readers a few useful tips too, e.g. *You should do the experiment over the sink!*

☞ Answers on page 154

14 When things go wrong

Quick fun

A rebus is a picture puzzle, e.g. REST / YOU'RE means YOU'RE UNDER ARREST.

Can you work out these other rebuses? Each one is something you might say in a problem situation.

1. MAN / BOARD
2. LOOK / KOOL
3. C YOURSELF YOURSELF YOURSELF YOURSELF
4. SHUT / SIT
5. YOUR TIME
6. ON THE / ON THE
7. LOOK
8. WATCH

Use this space to write out your topic words the first time. Use your own paper for extra practice.

Rewrite here those you had most trouble with.

Topic spelling list

damage	illegal
witness	escape
criminal	suspicious
arrest	poisonous
accidental	assault
difficult	robbery
problem	serious
disaster	emergency
disastrous	tragedy
dangerous	catastrophe
fatal	calamity

Arresting aid

When learning a word and copying it out, try to write the whole word in one go, rather than a few letters at a time. This will help build your 'visual memory' of the word.

Learn and write out the words from the **Topic spelling list**, remembering the tip. Try not to look back for each letter.

Fill in the gaps

Fill in the gaps with words from the **Topic spelling list.** Change the endings where needed.

1. Many snakes in Australia are extremely ____________________. Some bites will make you very sick but others can be ____________________.
2. Last night the police caught an ____________________ prisoner. For ten days the whole city had been living in fear because he was said to be very ____________________. He was wanted for a string of bank ____________________ and two vicious ____________________.
3. If you see any ____________________ activity you should report it to the police. The police can decide if anything ____________________ is going on. It is better to be safe than sorry.
4. Last year my uncle was a ____________________ to a burglary. As he acted quickly and rang the Triple 0 ____________________ number, the police arrived in minutes and an ____________________was made.
5. Last week was ____________________. First I destroyed our neighbour's favourite flowers and had to pay for the ____________________ even though it was ____________________ (my bike brakes failed). Then my brother and I got into ____________________ trouble playing a silly joke on our cousin.
6. Our last school camp was a bit of a ____________________. It rained all day, every day. We got bitten alive by mosquitoes. However, we forgot our ____________________ when the activities got under way. It's certainly more ____________________ to have fun in the pouring rain, but we still managed it!

Word scramble

Which words from the **Topic spelling list** are scrambled below?

1. MEADGA ____________________
2. OUSSREI ____________________
3. TYAREDG ____________________
4. SATRER ____________________
5. SATRESID ____________________
6. SASTALU ____________________

Killer words

Study these tricky words and tips and then write them without looking back.

awful	Remember: *I **saw** something **aw**ful.*	____________________
terrible	Learn with *horrible*.	____________________
worry	Use a spelling pronunciation to rhyme with *sorry*.	____________________
occurred	Say *occur-RED* to get the double ***r.***	____________________
happened	Say *happen-ED* to get the last bit right.	____________________
desperate	Say *des-PER-ate* to get the middle right.	____________________

Make up three sentences. Use two **Killer words** in each. Use your own paper.

Looking at … *ur*, *ir* and *er* words

The ***er*** sound is very tricky because it is spelt in many ways. The most common spellings are ***ur*** (*occ**ur***), ***er*** (*em**er**gency*) and ***ir***, (*f**ir**st*). A few words are spelt with ***or*** (*w**or**th*), ***ear*** (*s**ear**ch*) or ***our*** (*j**our**ney*).

The best idea is to learn the spellings of common words and use the dictionary when in doubt.

1. Learn the common words below, and look up the meanings of any you don't know. Then get Mum or Dad to test you.

er		***ur***		***ir***	
concern	deserve	burglar	further	stir	virtue
swerve	different	murder	murky	skirmish	mirth
mercy	nervous	turmoil	purpose	squirm	circle
personal	hermit	absurd	disturb	whirl	thirsty
alert	sermon	burden	surly	swirl	squirt

2. Which words from the box are part of these common expressions?

a You don't ______________ it.
b Shh! Please do not ______________.
c It's nothing ______________.
d Have ______________ on me.
e Patience is a ______________.
f Don't ______________ yourself.
g ______________ most foul!
h Don't ______________ things up.

3. Find the synonyms for these words from the box.

a awake ______________
b lecture ______________
c bad-tempered ______________
d humour ______________
e confusion, upset ______________
f ridiculous ______________
g unclear, muddy ______________
h small fight ______________

4. Look up the following words in your dictionary.

stern err dirge quirky curt lurch splurge curfew smirk

Which might you use to describe …

a a strict teacher? ______________
b a boring song? ______________
c a funny film or play? ______________
d a short reply? ______________
e a kind of movement? ______________
f a facial expression? ______________

Proofreading

Can you check this student's draft about his disastrous camping holiday?

Last holidays, my family went camping. It was an abslute catastrofee from start to finish. By the end of one weak, we were all desparate to get home. I'll go back to day one. The first problim was that a dangrous crimінel had escapt that day, and the police were everywhere. They serched every car, and talked to motorists to make sure they knew how serously danjerous this person was. They akst us to report anything at all that looked suspisious. We were all very frightend, but Mum told us not to wurry—she reckoned no one in their right mind would stop our car with four crazy kids in the back and everything but the kitchen sink on top! Anyway we saw nothing (we were quite disapointed ackshually) and we made it to our campsite near the beach.

Then our real trubbles began. First my baby brother trod on a poysonous snake! Luckyly the snake was more scarred than my brother and it slid away, but from then on, my mother was nurvous about every single thing. On the second day, my sister nearly drownd in the surf. She recuvered fairly quickly but we took her to the emirgency department anyway—an aweful experiense—worse than the acksident itself. All was quite for two days and then a real disastar struck. The tent fell down … in the middle of the night. Mum said this wouldn't have hapend if my father had checked the camping equipment. It only got wurse after that. We were all realy looking forward to getting back home but then—guess what—the police disided to block all the roads because the prisoner was still at large and had been seen in the area. We did finally get home, after one flat tyre and one fine for illegall parking. I don't think we'll be going camping again for a long, long time!

Vocabulary power

Some adjectives **go together with** certain nouns more than others do, e.g. it is common to say ***serious trouble*** but not so common to say ***severe trouble***.

1 Can you match the nouns in the box with the adjectives that go with them (**a**–**p**)? In most cases, there is only one possible match.

emergency	accident	robbery	circumstances	rescue	identity	suspect	verdict
escape	evidence	criminal	situation	bandit	damage	trouble	disaster

a	deep	______________	**b**	suspicious	______________
c	prime	______________	**d**	narrow	______________
e	nasty	______________	**f**	unanimous	______________
g	overwhelming	______________	**h**	man-made	______________
i	convicted	______________	**j**	armed	______________
k	masked	______________	**l**	tricky	______________
m	sudden	______________	**n**	mistaken	______________
o	dramatic	______________	**p**	permanent	______________

2 Now choose four adjective–noun pairs to use in sentences. Use your own paper.

Dictionary search

Use your dictionary to find the exact meanings of the words below. They all describe acts which break the law. Write down the meaning in your own words and then write the word to describe someone who commits this crime. You might have to ask a person to help you with the last task.

Illegal act	Meaning	Person who commits act
perjury		
manslaughter		XXXXXXXXXXXX
vandalism		
extortion		
blackmail		
treason		
slander		
arson		

Read and learn

You often need to 'picture' what is being written about in stories to understand new words and expressions. This story extract is about a boy, Snook, who has been allowed for the first time to go on his father's tuna boat. The extract begins as the boat collides with another. Picture the scene in your mind as you read.

… the violent unexpected lurch was enough to catch Snook unawares. For a split second he was off balance as he walked—one leg in mid-stride, hands free at his sides—and the boat's swerve did the rest. Like a bareback **buckjumper** thrown without a chance, he was tossed sideways before he could even grip handrail or **stanchion**; and the next moment he was hurtling over the side with a wide yell **in a pin-wheel confusion of arms and legs**.

…. Sam Snell glimpsed the falling body just before it hit the water and shouted **with the voice of a foghorn**, 'Snook!' he cried. 'Snook!' Then turning to the others, he yelled, 'Man overboard! Man overboard!

Snook's helpless tumble overboard had been one of the most frightening experiences of his life. He hit the water hard without a chance of drawing his breath, and the next instant he was being **pummelled** by waves and cross-currents as the **clipper**'s propellers **threshed** past him. He was spun about **like a rag doll**. The shock of the fall, the cold water engulfing him, the **seething din** in his ears, unnerved him so much that he started to **beat about blindly** with his arms. There was salt water in his mouth and nostrils and a great weight of sea above him. And then, just when the certainty that he was drowning began to fill his mind, he popped out on the surface and unconsciously took a gulp of fresh air. It saved him. Although he sank under water again the **buffeting** gradually **subsided** and he just had enough **presence of mind** to start swimming. After a few yards his head cleared and he paused, treading water and gasping like a **grampus**. The crisis was past; now he felt confident that he could stay afloat on the calm water without difficulty. At the same time he saw *Blue Fin*'s lights. They seemed a long way off …

Extract reprinted with permission from *Blue Fin* by Colin Thiele, Hachette Children's Books, 2000.

1 Answer the questions below about the words and images used in the story. The writer uses some terrific images. Write down what you see or hear for each image below.

a in a pin-wheel confusion of arms and legs (lines 10–11) ____________

____

b with the voice of a foghorn (lines 13–14) ____________

____

c like a rag doll (line 24) ____________

____

d beat about blindly (line 27) ____________

____

Do you know these words?

The nouns ***shemozzle*** and ***shambles*** are two great words to describe a mess, e.g.
*Despite all our hard work, the fete was a **shemozzle/ shambles** because of the heavy rain.*

2 Can you guess the meanings of these unusual words from the context?

a buckjumper (line 6) ____________

b stanchion (line 8) ____________

c clipper (line 22) ____________

d grampus (line 38) ____________

3 Circle the words which are closest in meaning to the words in the story. They are difficult words, but try to do it by using the clues in the text—don't use the dictionary just yet.

a	pummelled (line 21)	i	rolled gently	ii	hit repeatedly	iii	lifted
b	threshed (line 23)	i	beat	ii	sailed	iii	moved
c	seething din (line 25)	i	gushing water	ii	loud noise	iii	quietness
d	buffeting (line 34)	i	rough movement	ii	loud noise	iii	heaviness
e	subsided (line 35)	i	increased	ii	lessened	iii	moved away
f	presence of mind (line 36)	i	energy	ii	motivation	iii	ability to think

4 Now look up the words you were not sure of in your dictionary. Then look back at where they were used in the text.

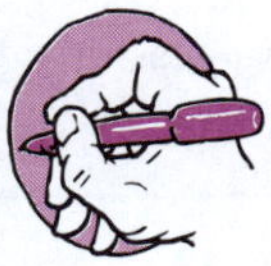

Your turn to write

Choose one of the following writing tasks. Before you begin, think about the plot, characters and setting, and do a rough plan of how the story will unfold. Use words from the unit—and your imagination, of course!

1 Write a story beginning *I knew something was wrong as soon as I …*

OR

2 Write a story beginning *It was the worst day of my life …*

OR

3 Write an imaginary newspaper report about a crime that happened in your town or suburb.

☞Answers on pages 154–155

15 Movies and television

Quick fun

How many words can you find in ENTERTAINMENT? Write your words in the box below but give yourself a time limit of 2 minutes or you'll never stop! (I found 40.)

Use this space to write out your topic words the first time. Use your own paper for extra practice.

Rewrite here those you had most trouble with.

Topic spelling list

review
comedy
drama
documentary
program
amusing
screen
script
visual
version
feature

original
reality
multimedia
channel
guide
episode
romance
animated
mythical
adaptation
sequel

Terrific tactic

If you are unsure about one or two letters in a word, write it on a scrap of paper, leaving a blank space for the letter. Try different letters in the space, e.g.

real_ty? ✗ *realety* ✗ *reality* ✓

Learn the words from the **Topic spelling list** and write them out. Use any strategies that work to remember the spellings.

Fill in the gaps

Fill in the gaps with words from the **Topic spelling list**. Change the endings as needed.

1. My friend and I attended a kids' film school in the holidays. We learnt all about making films starting with writing the ____________________.
2. We worked in groups to make a film—not long ____________________ films like those you see on the big ____________________—just little ones of about 5 minutes long. Of course, we had teachers to ____________________ us all the way.
3. One group made some clay figures and then moved them around to make the different scenes. They discovered how hard it was to make a good ____________________ film like *Wallace and Grommit*.
4. One group made a ____________________ film about people and their dogs. They plan to come again next holidays and make a ____________________—about people and their cats!
5. Some films were so funny. The most ____________________ one was about a ____________________ between two canaries. It wasn't meant to be a ____________________, but it was!
6. Our film was a serious ____________________ about friendship. Our ____________________ idea did not work out so we made three ____________________ before we were happy.
7. One day some people came from ____________________ Seven. They were looking for somebody to act in three ____________________ of a new drama series. They also asked if anybody was interested in taking part in a kids' ____________________ television program.
8. At the end of the two-week ____________________ we all had to ____________________ each other's work and give each other feedback. That was a bit embarrassing but we learnt some useful things.
9. Next holidays, we'll be old enough to do the basic ____________________ course. We'll learn about things like CD-ROMs that combine different media: written, ____________________, sound and film, for example.

Killer words

Study these tricky words and tips and then write them without looking back.

film	Only one syllable, so don't put a vowel before the ***m***.	____________________
video	You say the letter **e** (*vid***e***o*), so spell it with an **e**.	____________________
scene	Say *I see* (**c**) *a scene* to remember the **c**.	____________________
advertisement	Say *ADVERTISE-MENT* to remember the **e**.	____________________
effect	A noun meaning 'result', e.g. *special* ***effects***.	____________________
affect	A verb meaning 'influence', e.g. *rain* ***affects*** *attendance*.	____________________

Make up true sentences using the **Killer words**, perhaps combining them with words from the **Topic spelling list**.

____

____

____

Looking at … *ise* words

Many verbs of Latin origin are made with the suffix ***-ise*** (pronounced ***ize***), roughly meaning 'make' or 'do', e.g. *advert**ise***, *telev**ise***. (Some people prefer the spelling ***ize***, but ***ise*** is more common in Australian English.)

1 Learn these ***ise*** verbs and then get someone to test you on them.

dramatise	surprise	recognise	devise
criticise	apologise	organise	symbolise
despise	summarise	emphasise	idolise
improvise	analyse	mobilise	terrorise
revise	realise	disguise	categorise
supervise	memorise	modernise	mesmerise

2 Choose one verb which goes well with these nouns. (There may be more than one possibility.)

a ______________ schoolwork **b** ______________ a word

c ______________ a mistake **d** ______________ a plan

e ______________ a face **f** ______________ a story

3 Which of the words from the box could you use instead of the words in **bold** in the following sentences?

a There is no script to follow, so you'll just have to **make it up**. ______________

b First you must **work out the meaning of** the question. ______________

c The army had to **get** their troops **moving**. ______________

d Good performers can **send** you **into a trance**. ______________

e We have changed our school badge to **bring** it **up to date**. ______________

f Now the badge really **is a sign of** who we are. ______________

g My little brothers **look up to** my big brother and follow him everywhere. ______________

h **Sort out** the books into children's, teenagers' and adults'. ______________

Vocabulary power

Try to use precise, interesting words to express your **opinion** about film or television. It is boring to read *I liked/ I didn't like … the acting was good/bad …*, etc.

1 Can you put these verbs in rough order from strongest to weakest meaning. **Note**: you can do this in more than one way, but your answer should be similar to the one given.

a **liking:** *admire, love, enjoy, like, adore, be fond of*

strongest ______________

____

____

____

____

weakest ______________

b **not liking**: *dislike, loathe, hate, cannot stand/bear, do not care for, detest*

strongest ______________

____

____

____

____

weakest ______________

2 Now look at the words below meaning 'good' or 'very good'.

brilliant	able	fine	excellent	strong	awe-inspiring	competent	outstanding	
terrific	clever	classy	inspiring	good	unforgettable	memorable	impressive	capable

Can you categorise them into the following three groups?

Very strong approval	**Strong approval**	**Approval**

3 Think of some movies or TV programs you know, and write three **true** sentences about them using some words above. You might mention the actors as well. Use your own paper.

Proofreading

Can you check the spelling in these brief film reviews before they go to press?

March of the Penguins

Beautyful filumed documentery follows the incredable jerney of the Emperor penguins as they trek across Antartica to their traditionle breeding grounds. Recomended for all the family.

Lassie

Remake of the 1943 orijinal. A family financial crisis forces Joe to sell his belovd collie dog, Lassie, but the faithful dog ecsapes her new master and makes her way back to Joe. Take your tissues.

The Chronicles of Narnia

Based on the clasic novel by CS Lewis, this feeture film tells the tale of four children who travel through a wardrobe to the mystical land of Narnia and discuver it is their destiny to free the land. Brillient art direckion and special affecks.

Reminder
Use a thesaurus to help you think of interesting words to use.

Charlie and the Chocolate Factory

A young boy from a desparately poor family wins a tour through the biggest and best chocolate factory in the world, giuded by the weird and wonderful Willy Wonka. Wacky humor, bizarre caracters and outstanding performanses. Sure to be a movie favorit for years to come.

Read and learn

Reading other people's reviews will help you choose the words to use when writing your own. Read this extract from a movie review website, paying particular attention to the words in **bold**.

Your favourite movies

We asked you to tell us about your favourite movies of all time in 100 words or less. If you don't agree with these, let us know.

Harry Potter

As a **fanatical** fan of the *Harry Potter* books, I expected to be **transfixed** by the films—and I was. I knew the movie would not exactly match the images of the characters and places in my mind, but I needn't have worried. The 'baddies'—the **odious** Dursley family and the creepy Professor Snape amongst others—were vast improvements on my own imagination. A **gem**.

Star Wars

'A long time ago in a galaxy, far, far away…' So begins each of the six episodes in the *Star Wars* series, and with these words I am instantly **transported** into the fictional universe first created by George Lucas in 1977. This is what I love most about *Star Wars*: it is **literally** another world. Thank goodness Lucas did not stop after making the first three movies, and instead gave us three more—the '**prequels**'—set many years earlier and showing us the dark and mysterious origins of the terrifying Darth Vader.

Lord of the Rings

I was **sceptical** that anyone could successfully bring Tolkien's original **epic** tale to the screen, but I loved everything about Peter Jackson's **trilogy**. The very best thing was the computer-generated character, Gollum. Gollum was based on a real actor's performance and perhaps this is why he is so **mesmerising** as the twisted, **pathetic** character who struggles between his light side—helping the band of hobbits—and his dark side—wanting the ring (his 'precious') back in his own hands.

1 Choose the answers that are closest in meaning to the words a–j as they are used in the reviews.

a	fanatical	i	fantastic	ii	extremely enthusiastic	iii	crazy
b	transfixed	i	glued to my seat	ii	carried away	iii	delighted
c	odious	i	stupid	ii	pleasant	iii	hateful
d	gem	i	precious stone	ii	perfect	iii	rather good
e	transported	i	carried away	ii	caught a train	iii	glued to my seat
f	literally	i	actually	ii	like literature	iii	almost
g	sceptical	i	scared	ii	doubtful	iii	critical
h	epic	i	long	ii	interesting	iii	about great events and deeds
i	mesmerising	i	memorable	ii	hypnotising	iii	horrible
j	pathetic	i	deserving pity	ii	deserving hatred	iii	with no hope

2 a Look at the word 'prequels' and how it is used. Can you work out the meaning of the word and how it was formed? Write down your ideas. ______________________

____

b Do you know the meaning of the word 'trilogy'? Write down what you think it means and then check it in the dictionary. ______________________

____

Puzzle

1 Can you unscramble these different aspects of making films and television programs? They weren't all in the unit, but I'm sure you can work them out.

a DIONIRECT	____________	**b** UCTDORPION	____________
c STCAING	____________	**d** CEIALSP TEFFESC	____________
e PRISCTINGTWIR	____________	**f** TIDEGIN	____________
g TOGPHYEMARACIN	____________	**h** DOUSN	____________
i TINGLIGH	____________	**j** SPPRO	____________

2 Which words from the **Topic spelling list** am I thinking of?

a Hides a word meaning 'tear'. (6) ____________

b Hides a word meaning 'rug'. 8) ____________

c Hides a word meaning 'see'. (6) ____________

d Hides a word for a male sheep. (5) ____________

e Hides a word for a paper or file. (11) ____________

f Hides a two-letter pronoun. (7) ____________

g Hides a word for a great achievement. (7) ____________

Your turn to write

What is your favourite movie or television program?

Write a paragraph about it in about 100 words. Say what the movie or program is about (but don't give the whole story), and then write about one aspect that you especially like. It might be:

- the characters
- the imaginative story lines
- the special effects
- the humour
- or the way it makes you feel.

Look back at the **Read and learn** and **Proofreading** sections to get some ideas.

If you want, you could write 100 words about each—a movie and a television program. Remember to revise your writing carefully to be sure it makes sense.

☞Answers on page 156

Review 3

Now let's see what you remember of the words you learnt in Units 11 – 15. There are four tests in this review. You could do all in one session, or you could break them up and do them over a few days.

Step 1 Look at each group of words in the test and memorise them.

Step 2 Cover the five words up and test yourself (column 2). Try to do all five words in one go.

Step 3 Write your score out of 5 in the box. If you got any words wrong, go back and study them again.

Step 4 If possible, ask someone to test you on the words later—an hour or even a day later (column 3).

Test 1

Study	Test yourself	Test with another person
temperature iceberg blizzard remote glacier	/5	/5
discovered journey except compass advice	/5	/5
successful Antarctic accompany scientist fatigue	/5	/5
circumstance decide decision century peace	/5	/5
excellent precise scenery territory extreme	/5	/5
healthy diet energy muscle limb	/5	/5
	Total score = out of 30	Total score = out of 30

Test 2

Study	Test yourself	Test with another person
exercise physical activity stretch competition	/5	/5
champion frequent regular leisure stamina	/5	/5
protein sugar vitamin variety necessary	/5	/5
straight field observation investigate explanation	/5	/5
evidence evaluate materials hypothesis conclusion	/5	/5
disprove procedure survey dissolve mixture	/5	/5
	Total score = out of 30	Total score = out of 30

Test 3

Study	Test yourself	Test with another person
evaporate liquid exact separate contact	/5	/5
cause carefully task therefore expect	/5	/5
damage occurred arrest accidental difficult	/5	/5
disastrous dangerous illegal assault suspicious	/5	/5
serious catastrophe emergency happened desperate	/5	/5
concern deserve different nervous purpose	/5	/5
	Total score = out of 30	Total score = out of 30

Which word?

1. The terrible ________________ conditions stopped the expedition. (*desert, dessert*)
2. The explorers' ________________ took them right to the edge of the cliffs. (*root, route*)
3. What an extraordinary ________________! (*feet, feat*)
4. Most explorers kept detailed ________________ of their exploits. (*dairies, diaries*)

Test 4

Study	Test yourself	Test with another person
disturb circle awful terrible worry	/5	/5
review documentary program amusing sequel	/5	/5
version original disguise advertisement terrorise	/5	/5
episode film symbolise guide recognise	/5	/5
dramatise video criticise realise adaptation	/5	/5
memorise emphasise feature reality analyse	/5	/5
	Total score = out of 30	Total score = out of 30

5 If you ________________ your exercises, you might win. (*practise, practice*)

6 We think ________________ right. (*where, we're, wear*)

7 Bring ________________ swimmers. (*you're, your, yore*)

8 The children finished ________________ projects on time. (*they're, there, their*)

9 ________________ almost time to leave. (*Its, It's*)

Good work. I hope you did well with the **Which word?** section.

☞Answers on page 156

16 Strange happenings

Quick fun

How good are you at solving anagrams (unscrambling words to make new words)? In the puzzles below, the letters of each word group can be re-arranged to make something with a related meaning. For example, ASTRONOMERS can be re-arranged to make MOON STARERS.

Can you re-arrange the letters of these word groups to make a related idea?

1. THE EYES ____ ___ (**Hint**: what do eyes do?)
2. THE DETECTIVES ________ _________ (**Hint**: what detectives do)
3. TWELVE PLUS ONE _______ _____ ___ (**Hint**: middle word remains PLUS)
4. A DECIMAL POINT _'_ _ ___ __ ______ (**Hint**: the first word is I'M)

Use this space to write out your topic words the first time. Use your own paper for extra practice.

Topic spelling list

strange	imaginary
peculiar	extraterrestrial
supernatural	mysterious
alien	mystify
spirit	miraculous
monstrous	apparition
weird	behaviour
eerie	bizarre
psychic	grotesque
haunted	phenomenon (plural: phenomena)

Psychic strategy

Give yourself a challenge when learning spelling lists. Write the words from memory—in any order. You'll be concentrating so hard on remembering the words that you'll automatically get the spellings right.

Learn the words from the **Topic spelling list** and try out the strategy. How did you go?

Rewrite here those you had most trouble with.

Fill in the gaps

Fill in the gaps with words from the **Topic spelling list**. Change the endings as needed.

1. People say that 'truth is __________ than fiction' because the __________ of real, live human beings is often more surprising than that of __________ characters in books and films.
2. '__________' literally means 'outside earth'. '__________' can be used in the same way, but it can also mean 'foreigner'.
3. We were absolutely __________ by the woman's __________ behaviour.
4. I think cemeteries are __________ places, even in the daytime.
5. Everyone thinks our local cemetery is __________ because ten years ago some boys said they saw an __________ there—a woman in old-fashioned clothes and carrying a lantern. Of course she has become more __________ each time someone tells the story. I heard one version which said her face was __________ scarred.
6. I can't watch films and television programs about the __________ because I get too spooked.
7. Some __________ will always be __________ to humans because they can't be explained by scientific facts.
8. An old woman in the next street is said to be a __________. People often ask her to tell their future or to contact __________ of their ancestors. She looks a little __________, but she is really quite friendly and kind.

Killer words

Study these tricky words and tips and then write them without looking back.

invisible	Think of related words (*revise*, *vision*) to get the ***s***.	__________
ghost	Remember the spooky silent ***h***!	__________
extraordinary	Say this in two parts: *extra* and *ordinary*.	__________
lonely	Think of the base word *lone*. Then add ***ly***.	__________
unknown	Pronounce *UN-KNOWN*, not *UN-KNOWEN*.	__________
cemetery	Picture someone yelling ***e-e-e*** in fright to get the 3 **e**s.	__________

Write two sentences with three **Killer words** in each. Can you do it?

____

____

____

Looking at … the *x* sound

In English ***x***, ***cs***, ***ks*** and ***cks*** all sound the same, e.g. *wa**x**, shrie**ks**, hysteri**cs** and tri**cks***.

However, thinking about the meaning and noticing spelling patterns can help you get the right spelling, e.g. ***cs***, ***ks*** and ***cks*** are plural endings.

1. Learn the words below, and then get someone to test you. Take care with other words with an **x** sound.

x		***cs*, *ks* and *cks***		
waxing	flexible	chickenpox	hysterics	shrieks
mixed	next	perplexed	classics	spikes
mixture	text	context	graphics	flicks
relax	climax	complex	aerobics	specks
relaxation	reflex	prefix	politics	tricks
fixes	hoax	transfixed	athletics	fireworks

2. Which words might you use when talking about …

   a language and reading? ______________________

   b health and fitness? ______________________

   c something that surprises you? ______________________

3. Use the clues to fill in the chart below.

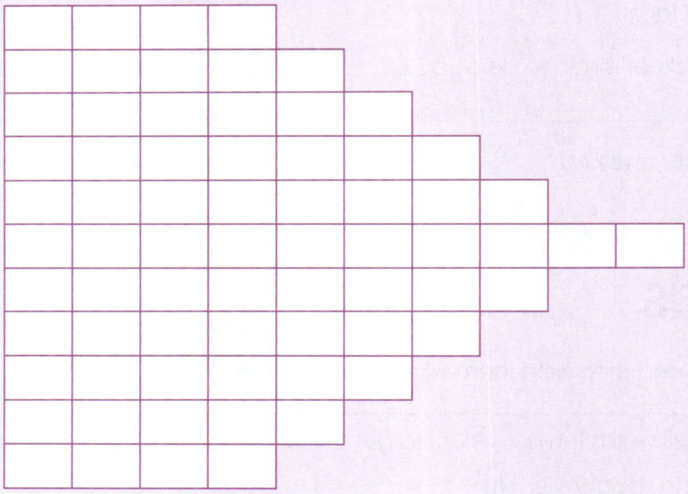

a Trick.
b Repairs.
c The most exciting part of a story.
d Cries out.
e Soft, supple.
f Unable to move.
g Drawings.
h Complicated.
i An automatic reaction.
j Following.
k Settle, quieten down.

Vocabulary power

1. There are many **idioms** you might use when talking about your reaction to **scary experiences**. Can you replace the missing words from the idioms below?

   a make your b _ _ _ d run cold

   b quake in your b _ _ _ s

   c be in a cold s _ _ _ t

   d scare someone out of their w _ _ s

   e be struck d _ _ b with fear

   f scare the living d _ _ _ _ _ _ _ s out of someone

g be a bundle of n _ _ _ _ s

h scare the p _ _ _ s off someone

i be on e _ _ e

j my heart was in my m _ _ _ h

2 Idioms like those above are similar to similes and metaphors. (Look back at Unit 8, **Read and learn**, if you are not sure about these.) They all use language in interesting ways to create an image of an idea or experience.

Can you make up your own creative expressions about fear to complete the sentences below? The idioms above should help give you ideas. The first one has been done for you.

a The sight of the face at the window *made my hair go straight*.

b As I opened the door, I was ______________________________.

c The silence only made things worse. We were scared ______________________________.

d I had never been so afraid. I felt as if ______________________________.

e I could not stop shaking. My nerves were ______________________________.

f I tried to scream out but my voice ______________________________.

g The sight was so ugly and revolting that ______________________________.

Proofreading

Can you see any mistakes in this poem draft?

The Unnowen

Spooks, spirrits, strang and errie things

Imaginery or reel? I don't know. Do you?

Sometimes at night, lonly in my room upstairs,

with the wind bloing and the rain on the windowpanes,

I'm sure they could egxist.

But when the sun shines the next morning: forget it.
No way.

Then visiting wierd old Mrs Fogarty's house on the hill,

near the old semetery,

I think again. Yep. I'm ready to beleve

It's hunted with all sorts of monsterous things.

Sure to be goasts in the bedrooms. Alians even.

Probably grotesk monsters too.

But back home, playing footy out the back: no. All
immaginary. Silly me.

Then I catch Mum watching *Supernaturel Tales* on
the telly.

A very peculyar look on her face. Extrordinary.

She looks almost green. Mmm. Maybe.

Then 'Make me a cup of tea, darling' she calls.

Back to the real world again.

Hey, what's that shreiking noise? Probably an owl.

But I might take my torch up to bed tonight anyway.

Just in case.

Read and learn

Stories about strange events often include vivid descriptions. These can give you good words and ideas to use in your own writing.

This extract is from a spooky story about a 13-year-old boy, Theo, who is recovering from a serious illness. Theo's family has just moved to a unit in a ten-storey block in a new suburb. The extract describes Theo's return to the unit after his first outing.

> Theo … felt that he'd be fine to walk up the stairs again, but he had promised his mother he'd go up in the lift. So he stepped into it. It, too, smelled of varnish, and new rubber flooring, and had gold lattice doors in an Oriental pattern, rather classy. He punched the button, and the lift moaned upwards.
>
> It was then that Theo noticed he was not alone in the lift. There was something crouched in the back corner against the wall. For the first three seconds Theo thought it was some weird bundle of yuk that someone had left there. Then he saw it pulsing slowly, like a sea anemone, and he realised it was alive.
>
> He was stunned. There was no other word for it. He couldn't even move away from it; he just stood there, freezing, staring. It was about the size of a medium dog, formless, as it if were made of three-quarters-set jelly. It looked rather like jelly too, with a faint sheen, almost but not quite translucent, like a slug. It was pearly grey, with darker, wet-looking areas.
>
> The bottom of it spread out, as if it had melted a little, and near where its chest might have been were two half-formed blobs like hands and paws. It was rounded on top, as if for a head, but this bit was turned away towards the corner.
>
> It gave off an unmistakable feeling of affliction and helplessness. A long shudder passed over it, and two semi-circular bulges on the front of what Theo thought was its head began to quiver, like eyelids about to open.
>
> Involuntarily Theo's mouth opened to let loose the kind of yell only heard in monster films, but all that came out was a croak. At that moment the lift stopped, the door wheezed open, and Theo stumbled out into the passage.
>
> The world turned spangly black. Dimly he heard the lift moaning downwards …
>
> From *Things in Corners* by Ruth Park.

Do you know this word?

The acronym ***ESP*** means ***extra-sensory perception***: the ability to know things without using the five senses (hearing, seeing, tasting, touching or smelling). The prefix ***extra-*** means 'outside' or 'in addition to'.

1. Which words in the story are used instead of those below?

   a beating ____________ **b** shine ____________

   c suffering ____________ **d** shake ____________

   e unintentionally ____________ **f** faintly ____________

2. What three things does the author compare the 'thing' to? ____________

3. From the image painted by the author, which of these words would you use to describe the 'thing'?
   threatening ☐ pathetic ☐ afraid ☐ eerie ☐ grotesque ☐ friendly ☐ evil ☐ (*tick the boxes*)

4. Which unusual verb is used to describe the movement of the lift in paragraphs 1 and 7? Why do you think the author chose this verb? ____________

   ____

5. The author says the doors of the lift 'wheezed open'. Do you think the doors opened quickly or slowly? Easily or with difficulty? ____________

   Why do you think the author chose this verb? ____________

6 In the last paragraph, what do you think it means that the *world turned spangly black*? ______________

____

7 On your own paper, draw what you think the 'thing' looks like, based on the vivid description in the extract.

Puzzle

See how you go with this unit crossword. Some clues are a bit cryptic—to fit the unit theme!

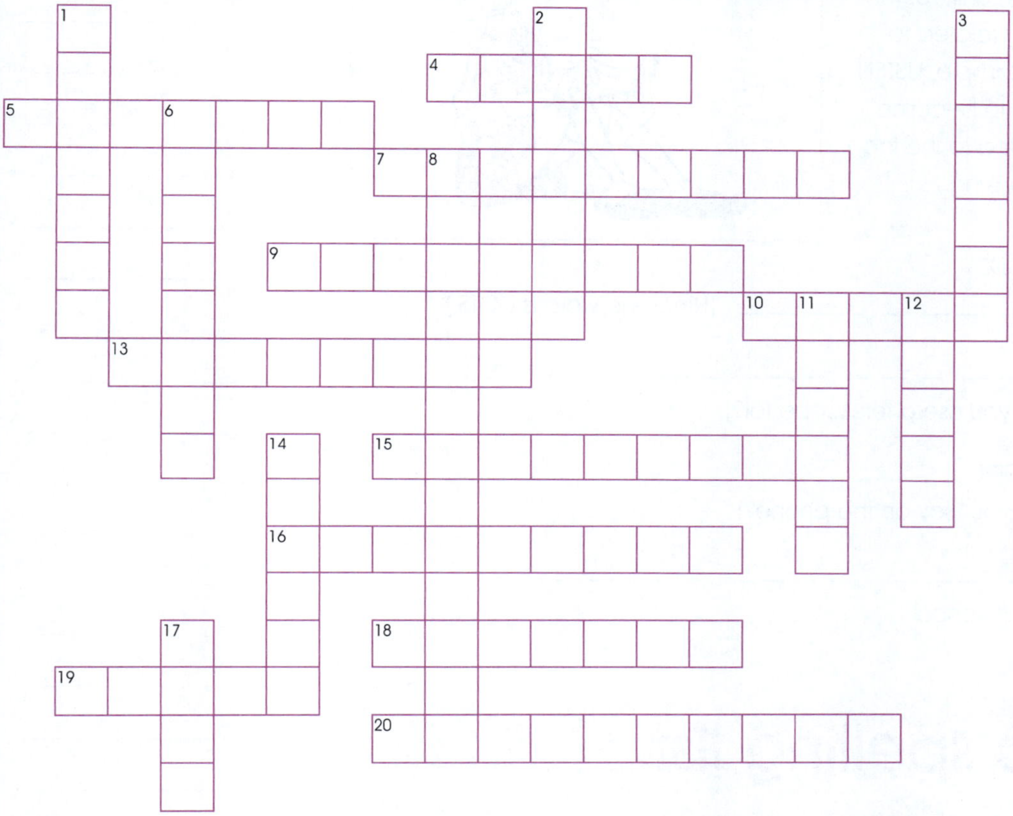

Across

4 Anagram of *wider*. (5)
5 Able to use ESP. (7)
7 Actions. (10)
9 You might have a fit of these if you see a ghost. (9)
10 Stranger from another land or world. (5)
13 This means strange and ends in *liar*. (8)
15 Extremely ugly to say the least. (9)
16 This can't be seen. (9)
18 Add ***a*** to a synonym of *chased* to get a word meaning chased by spirits. (7)
19 A spooky host. (5)
20 Full of mystery. (10)

Down

1 Perplex, puzzle. (7)
2 This sounds like a market or fete, but much stranger. (7)
3 This word hides *now*. (7)
6 A dead kind of place. (8)
8 Outside of the ordinary. (13)
11 Unhappy to be alone. (6)
12 It's hard to find a 5-letter word with more **e**s. (5)
14 Means 'energy and life', but also 'an unliving thing'. (6)
17 Trick. (4)

Your turn to write

Choose one of the following writing tasks. Be as imaginative and descriptive as you can. Try to use some words from the unit.

1 Write a story about a strange or unexplained experience. OR
2 Write a description of a supernatural or alien being. OR
3 Write a description of a scary or spooky place. OR
4 Write a poem about something strange or spooky.

☞Answers on pages 156–157

17 Machines and inventions

Quick fun

Here are some more anagrams for you to solve. As in Unit 16, the answer is something related to the first word. For example, LISTEN can be rearranged to become SILENT, which is related to the idea of listening and speaking.

1. THE MORSE CODE
   _ _ _ _ _ _ _ _ _ _ _ _ _ _ (**Hint**: one word is DOTS.)
2. A TELESCOPE _ _ _ _ _ _ _ _ _ _ _
   (**Hint**: what do you use a telescope for?)
3. A TELEPHONE GIRL _ _ _ _ _ _ _ _ _ _ _ '_ _ _ _ _'
   (**Hint**: what do you say on the phone?)
4. SCHOOLMASTER _ _ _ _ _ _ _ _ _ _ _ _
   (**Hint**: a place in school.)

Topic spelling list

motion
powered
force
engine
gear
pressure
effort
industrial
idea
fuel
device
forwards
backwards
automatically
battery
electricity
mechanical
manufacture
computerised
vehicle
vacuum
nuclear

Inventive idea

Try to visualise the word as you learn to spell it. Study it and then close your eyes. Can you still see it?

Try this out now with each word from the **Topic spelling list.** Use your other strategies as well, of course.

Use this space to write out your topic words the first time. Use your own paper for extra practice.

Rewrite here those you had most trouble with.

Fill in the gaps

Fill in the gaps with words from the **Topic spelling list**. Change the endings as needed.

1. An invention is something created by human __________ and intelligence, and which did not exist before. A simple example is the wheel.
2. Most inventions begin with a creative, original __________ to solve a problem.
3. A machine is a __________ built to do a particular job. Some machines are __________, converting one kind of energy to another—windmills, for example.
4. Many modern machines are __________: they depend on a silicon chip containing information and instructions to operate.
5. Many machines change the direction of the __________. When you ride a bicycle, your feet go round and round in a circular __________, but the bicycle moves __________ or sometimes __________.
6. Some simple machines are powered by muscles, but many need __________ such as coal or petrol to work. Most use __________ and bearings to run smoothly.
7. Some machines work by __________: squeezing air or liquid to create a force. Think of your bicycle pump or a roadworker's jackhammer.
8. In the middle of the 18th century, the __________ Revolution greatly changed the way people worked and lived. At first, machines to make work easier and faster were __________ by water, but then came steam power and the steam __________.
9. Most __________ these days is by machines even though this word originally meant 'made by hand' . Many factories use machines which operate totally __________.
10. In 1800, Alessandro Volta invented a device to produce __________, called a __________. Two hundred years later we are still using his same basic design to power everything from computers to watches.
11. Cars and other __________ these days depend more on computers to make them run.
12. __________ power is being used more in industry, but many people are against its use.

Killer words

Study these tricky words and tips and then write them without looking back.

purpose	Think of *purple* to get ***pur*** and then say ***pose***.	__________
several	Think of *sev**e**n* to remember the middle **e**.	__________
couple	Use a spelling pronunciation: *CO-UPLE*	__________
heavy	To remember the **ea**, say: *you h**ea**ve h**ea**vy things.*	__________
exist	There are no *eggs* in *e**x**ist*.	__________
improve	Learn with *move* and *prove*.	__________

Make up a sentence or two about a machine or invention—perhaps your own—using the **Killer words**.

Looking at … *au*, *augh* and *ough* words

The most common way to spell the **aw** sound is **or** (**or**der) and **aw** (dr**aw**). However, some words are spelt with **au** (c**au**se) or **augh** (c**augh**t). A small number are spelt with **ough**. Always check the dictionary if in doubt.

1 Learn these words and then write them out in alphabetical order. Use your own paper.

cause	haunted	audible	caught	ought
because	launch	caution	taught	bought
faulty	pause	exhaust	daughter	fought
fraud	sauce	saucer	haughty	nought
gauze	applaud	trauma	naughty	sought
haul	assault	saunter	slaughter	thought

2 Which words from the box are synonyms of the following words?

a should ____________ **b** attack ____________
c killing ____________ **d** take off ____________
e spooked ____________ **f** reason ____________
g broken ____________ **h** deceit ____________
i stop, halt ____________ **j** care ____________
k can be heard ____________ **l** plate ____________
m wicked ____________ **n** zero ____________

3 Look up the exact meanings of these words and then use them in your own short sentences.

a sought ____________
b applaud ____________
c haughty ____________
d saunter ____________
e haul ____________
f trauma ____________

Proofreading

Can you correct this student's unit spelling test? Warning: there are a few words from the last unit also. Write the corrections in the spaces.

meckanical	____________	effort	____________	computised	____________
powerd	____________	vehicle	____________	engine	____________
preshure	____________	couse	____________	backwoods	____________
cupple	____________	faulty	____________	automaticly	____________
divice	____________	thought	____________	purpos	____________
idea	____________	improove	____________	pause	____________
unknowen	____________	heavy	____________	caution	____________

sevral	________	doughter	________	behavyor	________
peckuliar	________	invisable	________	audible	________
force	________	batery	________	machine	________

Vocabulary power

Some words in the English language are actually **people's names**. For example, the Morse Code is named after its inventor, Samuel Morse. Even the word *America* comes from a person's name—Amerigo Vespucci—an Italian adventurer and navigator who sailed to the North and South American continents after Christopher Columbus.

1 Match the words in the box (derived from names) to the sentences. Use your dictionary if needed.

diesel	bloomers	pasteurisation	wellingtons	Fahrenheit	volt
watt	sandwich	boycott	Braille	Celsius	

a Footwear, also called gum boots, named after a British general who defeated Napoleon at the Battle of Waterloo

b Large, loose underpants for women, named after the American woman who designed them in 1850 for women to play sport in.

c Method of reading named after its blind inventor.

d Two ways of measuring heat, named after the scientists who invented them.

e Kind of engine and the oil used in it, named after its German inventor.

f Measurement of electrical power, named after the English inventor of the steam-engine. (You might see this word on a light bulb.)

g Another electrical measurement, named after its Italian inventor. (There's a clue in **Fill in the Gaps**.)

h Method of destroying bacteria in dairy products, named after the French scientist who invented it.

i Quick snack, named after an English earl who so loved playing cards that he wouldn't stop for lunch. Instead he got his servant to bring some meat between two pieces of bread.

j Word meaning to ignore or isolate someone because of bad behaviour, named after an English land agent who was so harsh to poor farm tenants, that no one would speak to him.

Did you know?

Many inventions and scientific discoveries were accidental. (Remember Archimedes in Unit 10?)

X-rays, vaccination and penicillin were all discovered accidentally. So too were many items we use every day: Post-it Notes, cellophane, Superglue, liquid paper and Velcro amongst others.

Velcro was invented by a nature lover who was always irritated by the burrs that stuck to his woollen pants when out walking. He investigated how the burrs were made—and Velcro was invented. So keep your eyes open and maybe you'll invent something important one day!

Read and learn

Read this information text about a special kind of machine, paying attention to the words in **bold**.

What do you see when I say the word 'robot'? Something like you and me perhaps, but metallic and making a beeping or whirring noise? Well, the fact is most robots are nothing like this at all.

A robot is a machine which is programmed by a computer to perform **specific** tasks—often tasks that are difficult, repetitive or dangerous. Robots can work for long periods without anyone supervising them. They have electronic sensors which see and feel the objects they are working with. These signals are passed onto the robot's control centre and then acted upon. This ability to respond to their environment **distinguishes** robots from all other machines.

We don't have to look too far to find examples of simple robots because many household devices work robotically. In other words, after being switched on, they work by themselves. Think of a dishwasher. It follows a program that you set when you press the start button, while you wander off to do more interesting things.

Far more complex robots are used in the world beyond the front door. In most car factories now, robots **assemble** the entire vehicle. In science, robots are used to **traverse** active volcano craters, something which would put vulcanologists' lives at great risk. Underwater robots are used to discover the secrets of the vast, permanently dark and bone-chillingly cold oceans.

Robots are of course essential to space exploration where **hazardous** conditions and rough **terrain** make it difficult or impossible for humans to function. Robotic rovers crawl over the surface of Mars and the moon taking rock samples from **inaccessible** areas. Others explore the outer **extremities** of our solar system, sending back information to scientists on planet Earth.

Some people wonder if robots will take over from humans one day. Sounds silly, doesn't it? But think about cars. Cars can now **monitor** traffic congestion and suggest alternative routes. Some models can override the driver's control in dangerous conditions and take action to avoid a crash—without the driver moving a muscle. How long will it be before a robot might actually drive the car, while the human driver sleeps or watches a movie in the back seat? Maybe it will even be able to drive without us being there at all: pop to the shops, pick up a take-away, or meet a family member at the station? Maybe the idea is not so **far-fetched** after all.

1 Choose the answers below that are closest in meaning to the words **a–j** as they are used in the text.

a	specific	i	special	ii	particular	iii	several
b	distinguishes	i	makes different	ii	makes special	iii	makes difficult
c	assemble	i	gather together	ii	put together	iii	meet
d	traverse	i	travel	ii	cross	iii	climb
e	hazardous	i	icy	ii	breathing	iii	dangerous
f	terrain	i	conditions	ii	people	iii	area of land
g	inaccessible	i	impossible to reach	ii	impossible to find	iii	far away
h	extremities	i	areas	ii	ends	iii	planets
i	monitor	i	watch	ii	avoid	iii	learn about
j	far-fetched	i	farthermost	ii	uncertain	iii	difficult to believe

2 Look up any other words you did not know in your dictionary. Then look up the words *android* and *humanoid*.

In which paragraph(s) is/are an android or humanoid robot mentioned? ______________________

Word scramble

Which words from the **Topic spelling list** are scrambled below?

1. CHEEVIL ____________________
2. SEERUPRS ____________________
3. CTTRICEELIY ____________________
4. SWOFDRAR ____________________
5. ABSWDARCK ____________________
6. WREDPOE ____________________
7. ANLACCMEHI ____________________
8. STARLIINDU ____________________

Puzzle

See how you go with this clueless puzzle. All the words are from the **Topic spelling list** or **Killer words**.

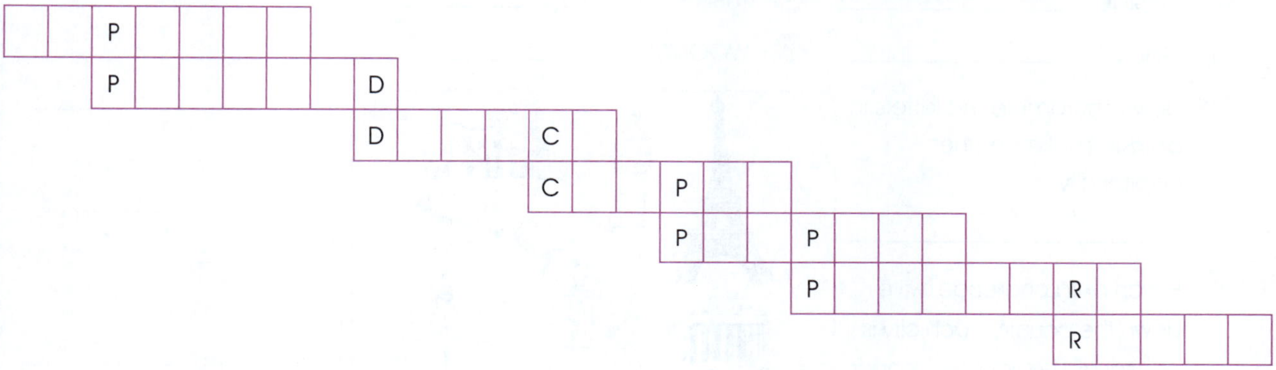

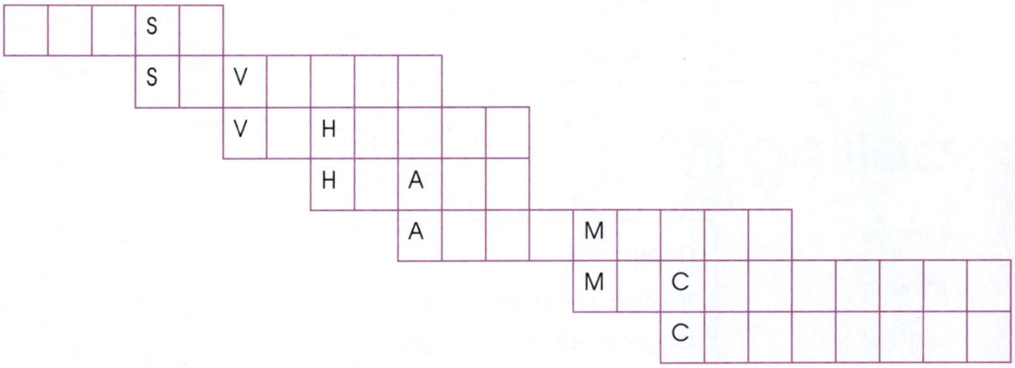

Do some Internet research to find out about inventions. Type in the name of the invention or the words *inventions* or *famous inventions*. You'll find plenty of interesting information.

Your turn to write

Choose one of the following writing tasks. Don't forget to revise and edit your writing.

1. Write about what you think is the most important invention of humankind, and why. Is it the computer? The safety pin? The wheel? The paper clip? The telephone? Or something else?

OR

2. Imagine you have invented an android. Describe what it looks like and what it does. Be imaginative—nothing is impossible!

☞ Answers on pages 157–158

18 Governing the country

Quick fun

Can you unscramble all these capital cities?

1. SP**AI**R ____________
2. SEANTH ____________
3. NOO**N**DL ____________
4. EM**RO** ____________
5. ONAHI ____________
6. ROI**C**A ____________
7. KKBO**A**NG ____________
8. D**R**IDAM ____________
9. JIBGIN**E** ____________
10. TU**B**IRE ____________
11. LABUK ____________
12. WOOMSC ____________
13. Now unscramble the letters in **bold** to make another capital city.

____

14. For an extra challenge, write down the country each city is capital of. Use your own paper.

Use this space to write out your topic words the first time. Use your own paper for extra practice.

Topic spelling list

law	premier
justice	minister
capital	parliament
mayor	represent
governor	representative
government	majority
council	political
councillor	participate
republic	monarchy
federal	constitution
electorate	democracy

Capital tip

Thinking of the base word in longer words can help you get the right spelling, e.g. thinking of *gover**n*** will help you remember the middle ***n*** in *gover**n**ment*.

Learn the words from the **Topic spelling list** using any strategies which help.

Rewrite here those you had most trouble with.

Fill in the gaps

Fill in the gaps with words from the **Topic spelling list.** Change endings and add capital letters as needed.

1. There are three levels of ________________ in Australia: federal, state and local.
2. At the local level, there are municipal and shire ________________. Elected ________________, led by the ________________, make decisions about local matters like streets, drains and libraries.
3. At the state level, elected representatives from each area or ________________ carry out the laws of the state. The leader of the state government is the ________________.
4. The ________________ government is located in the country's ________________ city, Canberra, and has responsibility for matters affecting the whole country: employment, the economy and immigration, for example.
5. Australia is a constitutional ________________. The king or queen of England has the supreme power, but this is limited by the country's ________________ (set of rules). Many people believe that Australia should become a ________________: where the people, through their representatives, hold supreme power.
6. The monarch's major ________________ in Australia is the ________________-General. This person has many powers but generally only acts on the advice of the Prime ________________.
7. Like many countries, Australia is also a ________________, a word from Ancient Greek. It means 'rule by the people' and gives the ordinary person the opportunity to ________________ in important decisions about the way the country is run. They do this by voting for someone to represent them in ________________.
8. People may vote for someone in a large ________________ party or for someone who is independent of any parties.
9. Both the police and courts administer the ________________ of the land. The courts decide if a law has been broken and if so, what should be done. They are concerned with ________________.

Killer words

Study these tricky words and tips and then write them without looking back.

people	Say *PEE-OH-PEE* to get the right vowel order.	________________
involved	Say *involv-ED*.	________________
together	Say *TO-GET-HER*.	________________
although	A hard one. Say it or write it out till you know it.	________________
service	Served with ***ice***?	________________
peace	This means quiet. Don't confuse it with *piece* (***pie****ce of* ***pie***).	________________

Make two sentences with three **Killer words** in each. Use your own paper.

Looking at … *ti* and *ci* words

The **sh** sound is sometimes spelt with a ***ci*** (*politi**ci**an*) or ***ti*** (*pa**ti**ent*). Many adjectives of Latin origin use this spelling and you can sometimes work out if it is a ***ci*** or ***ti*** by looking at the base word, e.g. *office* ➝ *offi**ci**al*, *part* ➝ *par**ti**al*.

1. Learn these ***ci*** and ***ti*** words. Ask someone to test you on them.

***ci* words**			***ti* words**	
official	racial	politician	cautious	partial
artificial	financial	ancient	fictitious	essential
social	precious	sufficient	initiate	confidential
commercial	suspicious	efficient	patient	potential
special	delicious	appreciate	initial	torrential

2. Find the antonym (opposite) of these words from the box.

a modern ____________ **b** complete ____________
c ordinary ____________ **d** natural ____________
e true ____________ **f** final ____________
g daring ____________ **h** worthless ____________
i unnecessary ____________ **j** not enough ____________

3. Which words from the lists could be used in these phrases?

a a _____ci_____ meal **b** have _____ti_____ to do well
c _____ci_____ gems **d** _____ti_____ a project
e _____ti_____ rain **f** an _____ci_____ system
g a _____ci_____ event **h** make an _____ci_____ announcement
i _____ci_____ background **j** the _____ci_____ district
k a _____ti_____ secret **l** _____ci_____ your kindness

Dictionary search

Use your dictionary or thesaurus to find these ***ci*** words.

1. MAL____________ very evil
2. CR____________ very important
3. PRO____________ very able
4. DEF____________ lacking
5. VI____________ savage
6. ASS____________ club, union

Read and learn

When reading about 'big ideas', such as ways of government, you will often meet new words. Always try to make a rough guess at meanings using the context **before** looking in the dictionary. Read this information text. Don't look up any words just yet.

How did democracy originate?

Democracy is a system of government in which everybody has a say in the way the country is run. It can be direct, where everyone helps to make every decision, or representative, where groups of people choose or vote for someone to represent them when important decisions are being made. Direct democracies are not practical for modern countries. It is just not possible to gather everyone together every time an important decision is to be made.

The word democracy comes from the Greek language and means rule by the people: *demo* meaning people and *kratia* meaning rule. The word was **coined** to define the system of government in Athens in around 500 BC.

The democracy of early Greece was a direct democracy. This was possible because the ruling class of citizens was only small so it was quite easy to get everyone **eligible** to vote together in one place. Most of the people were slaves and they, together with women and foreigners, had no right to vote or **hold office**. This system, which placed power in the hands of an **elite** group and excluded the bulk of the **populace**, would not qualify as a democracy today.

The modern world owes a great deal to the ancient Greeks **nevertheless**. It also owes much to the Middle Ages. During this period, the idea **evolved** that there was a contract between a ruler and his or her subjects and both sides **were obligated** to perform certain duties. If a ruler did not, the people had a right to take back his or her powers. The idea of representation also began in these times.

An essential aspect of democracy is that the voting is by **secret ballot** so that everyone can vote however they want. Also, voting is carefully **monitored** to ensure it's a fair process. This was not always the **norm**. In the 19th century, it was highly **controversial**. It was widely felt that no-one would want to keep his vote secret unless he was ashamed of it!

1. Now read the text again and write a rough meaning for each word in **bold** in the table below. Then use your dictionary to check how close you were, and write the exact meaning down in note form.

Word from text	Your rough guess at meaning	Dictionary meaning
a coined		
b eligible		
c hold office		
d elite		
e populace		
f nevertheless		
g evolved		
h were obligated		
i secret ballot		
j monitored		
k norm		
l controversial		

2. Look up any other words you did not know.

Proofreading

Can you correct the spelling mistakes in this student's recount? Remember there could be mistakes in words from other units in the book.

Our class travelled to our nashional cappital, Canberra, last week to learn about goverment and politicks. We visited many diffrent places but the most intresting was Parlament House. It was very eggsiting to be standing in the acksual building wear the Prime Minster, Leader of the Opposition and minsters work and make importent dicisions on our behalf. We first went into the Great Hall, where many offitial funcktions and speshial sociall events are held. I thaught it was absolutly beautiful, espeshially the extrordinary tapestry of the Australian bush. We then walked to the House of Representives and the Senate. The guide explaned the different pirpose of the two chambers and pointed out where everyone would sit. We met the fedral representive for our electrate, Mrs Karen Brinker, and she talked to us about how bills were passed to change lows. She also discused the opportunitys poeple had to particpate in the process of goverment in a democrasy, beginning with voting at eleckions—at federal, state or local counsel level. Although we did more fun activitys on other days, I enjoied this day the most. It made me appresiate how many people were involvd in running the country and how much work they do.

Vocabulary power

We can see **Greek or Latin origins** in many words used to talk about government, e.g. ***democracy*** is made up of the Greek word roots ***demo*** meaning 'people' and ***kratia*** meaning 'rule'—so, rule by the people. In Unit 2, we looked at the Latin–Greek root ***pol*** (meaning 'citizens' or 'city') in words like ***political*** and ***politician***.

1. Study these other important word roots:
   civis meaning 'citizen' ***sent*** meaning 'feel' ***dic/dict*** meaning 'say' ***reg*** meaning 'rule'
   cap meaning 'head' ***vol/volv*** meaning 'turn' ***unus*** meaning 'one' ***populus*** meaning 'people'

2. Can you work out these words derived from the word roots above?

a	Non-military person.	CIV _ _ _ _ _	**b**	Not primitive.	CIV _ _ _ _ _
c	Thoughtful, reasonable.	SEN _ _ _ _ _	**d**	Silly ideas or words.	_ _ _ SEN _ _
e	Tell the future.	_ _ _ DIC _	**f**	Ruler with total power.	DIC _ _ _ _ _
g	Royal.	REG _ _	**h**	Army unit.	REG _ _ _ _ _
i	Boss, chief.	CAP _ _ _ _	**j**	Main city.	CAP _ _ _ _
k	Go around.	_ _ VOL _	**l**	Turn against.	_ _ VOL _
m	Bring together as one.	UN _ _ _	**n**	Only one, special.	UN _ _ _ _
o	Well-liked.	POP _ _ _ _	**p**	Number of people.	POP _ _ _ _ _ _ _

Puzzle

How many words from the unit can you find here? The words may appear diagonally as well as horizontally and vertically.

C	A	T	C	O	G	O	R	S	P	S	K	S	O	F	F	I	C	I	A	L
O	M	A	O	H	K	F	A	T	J	R	S	E	S	H	E	D	X	O	P	Y
U	A	I	U	S	Q	F	Y	O	R	W	E	X	Z	T	J	E	P	F	P	G
N	Y	U	N	B	J	I	C	G	V	Z	R	M	D	N	K	M	A	V	R	W
C	O	F	C	I	U	G	X	E	I	D	V	V	I	U	U	O	R	L	E	M
I	R	E	I	B	S	P	T	T	C	F	I	A	G	E	T	C	T	P	C	C
L	P	O	L	R	T	T	W	H	W	L	C	O	F	I	R	R	I	V	I	A
P	S	A	L	R	I	B	E	E	P	Q	E	U	H	R	R	A	C	E	A	P
A	Q	C	O	M	C	U	W	R	E	P	U	B	L	I	C	C	I	M	T	I
P	Y	Q	R	Q	E	M	A	Y	U	E	F	I	E	J	V	Y	P	O	E	T
A	C	O	U	N	C	I	I	C	P	O	L	I	T	I	C	I	A	N	W	A
R	E	L	E	C	T	O	R	A	T	E	E	F	V	C	L	K	T	A	A	L
L	S	R	E	R	E	P	R	E	S	E	N	T	A	T	I	V	E	R	L	I
I	S	I	G	O	V	E	R	N	M	E	N	T	F	D	C	Q	K	C	T	N
A	E	N	N	N	P	R	M	X	H	Y	F	E	D	E	R	A	L	H	H	V
M	N	H	Y	D	E	Q	D	O	W	T	C	P	V	M	O	Z	P	D	O	O
E	T	M	P	S	O	Y	L	G	M	P	J	P	S	O	C	I	A	L	U	L
N	I	F	E	D	P	L	E	I	K	A	Y	E	L	Z	J	N	T	I	G	V
T	A	D	Z	J	L	F	V	U	G	R	R	A	M	P	C	D	I	M	H	E
O	L	A	W	P	E	A	C	E	D	L	Z	F	M	A	A	E	E	O	G	D

Did you know?
The word ***Canberra*** is from an Aboriginal word meaning 'meeting place'.
The word ***parliament*** is from a French word meaning 'speaking or discussing'.

Your turn to write

Choose one of the following writing tasks. Ask a parent or friend for help with the first one if you need to. Remember to revise your writing carefully.

1. Write a report about the government of the area you live in. You could cover all levels of governments or just one. Be sure to include information about your electorate and representatives. OR
2. What would you do if you were in charge of your council area, state or territory? Or the whole country? Over to you!

☞ Answers on pages 158–159

19 Out in space

Quick fun

Can you turn SPACE to SCOPE in eight steps? Use the clues and change one letter each time. What about MOON to HEAT? And MARS to CONE?

1. SPACE

   _ _ _ _ _ _ (extra)

   _ _ _ _ _ _

   STARS

   _ _ _ _ _ _ (wounds)

   _ _ _ _ _ _

   _ _ _ _ _ _

   SCOPE

2. MOON

   _ _ _ _ (groan)

   _ _ _ _

   _ _ _ _

   HEAT

3. MARS

   _ _ _ _

   _ _ _ _

   _ _ _ _

   CONE

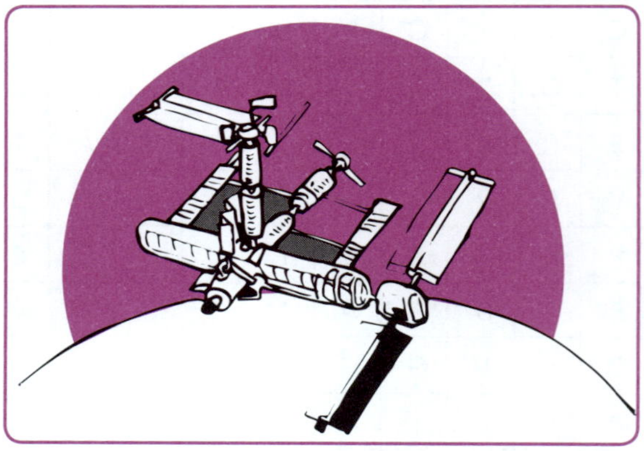

Topic spelling list

orbit	astronaut
planet	constellation
astronomer	universe
satellite	telescope
shuttle	asteroid
launch	oxygen
comet	hydrogen
galaxy	capsule
gravity	elliptical
collapse	astrology
eclipse	meteorite

Supersonic strategy

Remember: breaking longer words into syllables will help you avoid missing out letters or even whole syllables, e.g. *AST-RO-NOM-ER, MET-E-OR-ITE*.

Break the words from the **Topic spelling list** into syllables and then write them out.

Of course, you can use other strategies as well.

Use this space to write out your topic words the first time. Use your own paper for extra practice.

Rewrite here those you had most trouble with.

Fill in the gaps

Fill in the gaps with words from the **Topic spelling list.** Change endings and add capital letters if needed.

1. Most scientists believe that the ______________ came into being about 15,000 million years ago with a gigantic explosion called the Big Bang.
2. Using radio-______________, ______________ have found background 'radio' noise which they say is an echo of the Big Bang.
3. When Isaac Newton observed an apple falling to the ground, he realised it was because of the Earth's 'pull' or '______________'.
4. A ______________ is a group of stars that we can see in a particular part of the night sky.
5. A ______________ is a much larger group of stars—like an island of stars in the vast ocean of space. Our solar ______________ is in one called the Milky Way.
6. The Sun, like all stars, is an immense ball of glowing gases—mainly ______________ and helium.
7. When one heavenly body, like the Moon, passes in front of another, like the Sun, an ______________ occurs.
8. ______________, ______________ and ______________ are smaller bodies which travel through space, sometimes entering the Earth's atmosphere.
9. Black holes occur when massive stars ______________ and create a solid area from which no light can escape.
10. Russian ______________ are called cosmonauts, but their work is the same.
11. ______________ are large, spherical bodies which ______________ the Sun or other stars in an ______________ pattern.
12. The ______________ is the compartment in a rocket where astronauts live during flights.

Killer words

Study these tricky words and tips and then write them without looking back.

farther	Think of the base word *far*.	______________
further	Learn with *f**ar**ther*. Only one letter is different.	______________
maximum	Three syllables. Remember: *mum* is at the end.	______________
minimum	Same as above.	______________
system	Think of *m**y** s**y**stem* to remember the ***y***.	______________
entire	Learn with *fire*, *wire* and *hire*.	______________

Make two sentences with three **Killer words** in each, or if that does not work, three with two in each.

____

____

Looking at … *ite* and *ity* words

Some words ending in ***ite*** have a long ***i*** sound (*satellite*). Others have the *schwa* (**eh**) sound (*defin**ite***). Words ending in ***ity*** also have the *schwa* sound (*gravity*).

1 Learn the words below and then write them out in alphabetical order. Try to write each word in one go without looking back for each letter.

Reminder
We don't hear the vowel sound clearly in unstressed syllables. Instead we hear the *schwa* (*eh*).

***ite* (long *i* sound)**		***ite* (*schwa* sound) and *ity***			
satellite	parasite	definite	exquisite	purity	curiosity
meteorite	stalactite	favourite	granie	charity	equality
appetite	stalagmite	hypocrite	personality	security	infinity
dynamite	graphite	infinite	hostility	similarity	humanity
finite	ignite	opposite	insanity	authority	facility

2 Which word am I thinking of?

a A hard type of rock.

b This is found in pencils.

c A kind of animal.

d Found on a cave ceiling.

e Madness.

f Going on forever.

g This killed the cat.

h This makes a big bang.

i Sure.

j Very fine, beautiful.

3 Use your dictionary if needed to find the word above which means …

a a person who pretends to believe something.

b a feeling of hate between two people or groups.

c people in general, or respect for people in general.

d limited, having an end.

Proofreading

Can you correct this student's draft for a project on space?

Facts and figures about space

- There is now one less planit in our solar sistem. In 2006, the world's sientists desided that Pluto did not quolify as a planet.
- There are no limets to the Univers. It is just that we don't have telerscopes powerfull enuff to obsirve it all.
- Our galacksy, the Milky Way, has more than 200 million, million stars.
- Humans have allways looked to the skies, but the Greeks were the first astronmers to record their obsirvations.
- The first astronat in spase was a Russian, Yuri Gagarin, on April 12 1961.
- Our sun looks like the biggest star in our solar system, but that is only because the other stars are much father away.

- To break Earth's gravety, space shuttels must generate more power than 140 Boeing 747 aeroplanes.
- The word satelite means 'attendant' and refers to natural and man-made bodies that orbet others in space.
- We think of solar eclipsses as unusual, but they ackually occer somewhere on the planet about once every six months.

Vocabulary power

We often make **adjectives** from nouns and verbs, e.g. by adding ***ic***, ***al***, ***ical***, ***ous***, ***eous*** or ***ly***. Often we need to change a few final letters, e.g. *univers**e*** → *univers**al***, *circl**e*** → *circul**ar***.

1 Can you make adjectives from these words AND get the spelling right? You might need to use your dictionary for some.

a	astronomy	______________	**b**	astrology	______________
c	meteor	______________	**d**	atmosphere	______________
e	orbit	______________	**f**	galaxy	______________
g	telescope	______________	**h**	planet	______________
i	dynamo	______________	**j**	nucleus	______________
k	ellipse	______________	**l**	globe	______________
m	robot	______________	**n**	gas	______________
o	heaven	______________	**p**	gravity	______________

2 Some adjectives are quite different from their noun counterparts because they have different origins. Do you know the adjectives from these words?

a	sun	_ _ _ AR	**b**	moon	_ _ _ AR
c	star	_ _ _ _ _ AR	**d**	sound waves	_ _ _ IC

3 Now look up *celestial* in your dictionary. Which adjective from **1** above is it closest to? ______________

Dictionary search

There are many adjectives we can use to describe the size of objects and distances in the universe. Try to use these instead of always using *very big* or *very small*.

1 Look up these words and then write them in the correct spaces below. Before you do, guess their meaning and write ***B*** for **big** or ***S*** for **small** next to each.

minute (____)	infinitesimal (____)	gargantuan (____)	mammoth (____)
microscopic (____)	colossal (____)	minuscule (____)	diminutive (____)

a **very small** ______________________________

b **very large** ______________________________

2 Now choose four to use in your own sentences about space. Use your own paper.

3 What other words do you know for …

a very big? ______________ **b** very small? ______________

Did you know?

The International Space Station (ISS) is the largest, most ambitious construction project humankind has ever attempted. It is actually being built in space. The ISS is like a little city orbiting the Earth. It is constantly manned, and so provides a permanent human presence in space. It takes 90 minutes to do a complete orbit and circles the Earth 16 times a day. When finished, it will be the third brightest object in the sky after the Sun and the Moon. You can see the ISS in the night sky now but you need to find out on the Internet when it will be visible in your area.

Read and learn

Check out the Internet for more information about the ISS and the fascinating world of outer space

1 Some words are missing from the text below. Read the article right through, thinking about what the missing words could be.

So you'd like to be an astronaut?

Travelling in space looks like a lot of fun, doesn't it? But have you thought about what it would be like living for long periods of time in space—like the International Space Station astronauts right now?

First of all, for twelve hours each day these astronauts are hard at work. They might be checking equipment and systems, **(a)** ____________________ experiments, or communicating with ground control. They might be on a space-walk, doing highly dangerous repairs to the **(b)** ____________________ of the station. When they are not working, they are exercising—for about two hours each day. Microgravity can cause muscles and bones to weaken and **(c)** ____________________ so regular exercise is crucial.

Eating is easier for astronauts than it used to be. No more is the astronaut's diet restricted to chicken-feed **(d)** ____________________ of bland, tasteless, freeze-dried food. Now they select their own menus under guidance from nutritionists, but many foods still have to be **(e)** ____________________, as water is too heavy and expensive to carry within foods. Of course, this means that all **(f)** ____________________ are in powdered form too. So it is still likely that eating and drinking get a little **(g)** ____________________.

Even breathing is a challenge on the space station, and managing the air supply is critical. Take the enclosed, **(h)** ____________________ quarters, and up to seven people at a time breathing in the air, as well as breathing out carbon dioxide and small amounts of **(i)** ____________________ gases like ammonia. Add smells and gases from scientific experiments, and you can see the problem.

Astronauts also have to deal with the idea that they may be drinking water recycled from other crew members or even laboratory **(j)** ____________________ (yes, I mean rats)! The Space Station has to produce water itself—**(k)** ____________________. It is too expensive to transport, so they recycle everything, including water from teeth-cleaning, hand washing, and, yes, even urine. They also use the water lost through **(l)** ____________________ and sweating. These all add to the cabin humidity which is eventually condensed and returned to the water supply. Still like the idea of travelling in space?

After all that hard work, astronauts need a good sleep, and they get one. However, because space is tight and there is no gravity, they might have to sleep anywhere—as long as they find something to hook up to, so they won't just float away.

On top of all this, astronauts have to deal with the very real **(m)** ____________________ that something will go wrong, and they will not return to their planet and loved ones. A pretty tough job all round, I would say.

2. Now choose a word from the box to write in each space above. Do the ones you are sure of first and only use your dictionary if you are really stuck. After you check your answers, look up the meaning of any words you do not exactly understand.

exterior	pellets	indefinitely	rodents	monotonous	exhalation	monitoring
prospect	atrophy	rehydrated	beverages	noxious	cramped	

Puzzle

1. Which words from the **Topic spelling list** or **Killer words** hide the words below?

   a. A word for a sphere. (5) orbit (contains ***orb*** which means 'sphere')

   b. A part of the mouth. (7) __________

   c. A word for say or relate. (9) __________

   d. A word for close. (7) __________

   e. A head covering. (7) __________

   f. A part of a poem or song. (8) __________

   g. The past tense of *meet*. (5 or 9) (two possible answers) __________

   h. A word meaning 'lace'. (6) __________

   i. A word meaning 'a special event'. (6) __________

   j. A short word for police. (9) __________

   k. A word meaning 'mother'. (8) (two possible answers) __________

   l. An animal covering. (7) __________

   m. A part of a plant. (6) __________

2. Which word …

   a. can you take one letter from and get a meal? (6) __________

   b. can you take one letter from and get a parent? (7) __________

   c. can you take one letter from and get a dangerous drug? (8) __________

Your turn to write

Choose one of the following writing tasks.

1. Imagine you are on the International Space Station, or any spacecraft. Write about your day, using the information in this unit, especially the **Read and learn** section, and lots of your own imagination. You might write about your whole day, as in a diary, or just one episode.

OR

2. Write a report about one aspect of space: planets, stars, galaxies or something else you are interested in. Plan your writing first and begin with a definition of your subject.

☞Answers on pages 159–160

20 Behave yourself!

Quick fun

Use the letters in the box below to make as many words as you can. Each word must have at least 3 letters and contain ***R.*** Can you see one nine-letter word relating to the unit theme? (10 words is good and 20 or more is fantastic!)

E	L	A
C	R	O
T	E	N

____

____

____

Topic spelling list

fair	loyal
forgive	prejudice
honour	tolerance
honest	generous
truthful	co-operate
value	trustworthy
thoughtful	virtue
quality	courageous
charity	conscience
knowledge	guilty
accepting	innocent

Trusty tip

An excellent way to improve your spelling and word knowledge is to do crosswords and puzzles and play word games like *Scrabble* and *Boggle*.

By now you know lots of strategies to remember words. Use them on the words from the **Topic spelling list** as you write them out.

Use this space to write out your topic words the first time. Use your own paper for extra practice.

Rewrite here those you had most trouble with.

Word scramble

Which words from the **Topic spelling list** are scrambled below?

1. TRUEVI ______________
2. RONOUH ______________
3. STONHE ______________
4. RATHCIY ______________
5. GRIFEVO ______________
6. UGREENSO ______________

Fill in the gaps

Fill in the gaps with words from the **Topic spelling list**. Change the endings as needed.

1. The word '________________' can mean 'doing good deeds for others' or 'an organisation that does good deeds for others'.
2. Dad says my sister and I need to ________________ more when we have to do the household chores, instead of arguing all the time about what is ________________ and what is not.
3. If you are ________________ of some wrong-doing, it is best to be ________________ and ________________ and own up.
4. Your ________________ tells you what is right and wrong.
5. It is very ________________ of my great-grandmother to remember my birthday, seeing she has 20 great-grandchildren. When I was born, she started a bank account for me with a very ________________ amount of money.
6. My big brother has many ________________, but being ________________ when someone has offended him is not one of them.
7. Mum says we are very responsible and ________________ now, so she lets us go on the train to the movies.
8. The things we ________________ are the things we care a lot about.
9. Dogs are said to be very ________________ pets—faithful to their masters forever.
10. The old man who came to our ex-students' day said it was an ________________ to meet us all and see our young smiling faces.
11. If we were all more ________________ and ________________ of differences, the world would be a happier place.
12. '________________' means 'pre-judging'—judging people before you know anything about them. ________________ and education is the only way to beat this problem.

Killer words

Study these tricky words and tips and then write them without looking back.

wrong	Don't forget the silent ***w***.	________________
learn	Remember: you use your ***ear*** to *l**ear**n*.	________________
happiness	Remember: the middle letter is ***i*** not ***y***.	________________
succeed	Two ***c**s* and two ***e**s*.	________________
properly	Say the 3 syllables to remember the ***er***.	________________
goodbye	This seems easy, but don't forget the final **e**.	________________

Try to use all six of the **Killer words** in one sentence. I'm sure you can do it. Use your own paper.

Looking at … apostrophe review

We use the apostrophe for two reasons:

- to show a letter is missing, e.g. *doesn't*. The apostrophe shows that the letter **o** is missing (*does n**o**t*).
- to show that one person or thing has ownership or possession of another, e.g. *Harry's mother* or *the mother of Harry*. The apostrophe of possession always goes directly after the thing that does the owning. Look back to **Apostrophe of possession** (page 72) if you are not sure.

In this last chapter, we will do a review of both kinds.

1 Add apostrophes where needed in the following sentences. Don't just put an apostrophe when you see a word ending in **s**. Think about whether or not somebody 'owns' something else.

- **a** Nelsons family is getting ready for a big party.
- **b** Hes been very sick for two weeks and probably shouldnt go, but he doesnt want to miss it.
- **c** Its a really big occasion: his grandparents sixtieth wedding anniversary.
- **d** All his cousins and his cousins cousins will be there.
- **e** He will meet his grandfathers brother for the first time.
- **f** His three aunties and uncles from Darwin will be there. They havent even met Nelsons little brothers.
- **g** His youngest sisters favourite person in the whole world will be there. Shes coming all the way from Perth.
- **h** The party will be held at his grandparents house in Adelaide. Its a long way to travel for most people but theyre all coming.
- **i** Therell be a jumping castle for the little children, but the older children will have to help out with serving food and drinks.
- **j** Nelson hasnt seen his grandparents for three years, so its important to them all that he attends.

2 Which troublesome contractions are muddled here?

a	'SODTEN	________	**b**	SHA'NT	________
c	V'AHNET	________	**d**	NDITD'	________
e	DSOHLUNT'	________	**f**	WREENT'	________

Proofreading

Can you check this student's spelling test? There are quite a few mistakes to find.

carm	________	rather	________	fasinating	________
coperate	________	curadgeos	________	thortful	________
quolity	________	knowledge	________	honur	________
honest	________	fair	________	loil	________
proply	________	charety	________	predjudice	________
valyou	________	genrous	________	theyre	________
vertew	________	conshence	________	sistem	________
several	________	happyness	________	lern	________
truthfull	________	havent	________	toleranse	________
further	________	collapse	________	definate	________
forgiv	________	acksepting	________	suceed	________

Vocabulary power

We make **nouns** from adjectives using suffixes like ***-ness***, ***-ship*** and ***-y***. Remember to change ***y*** to ***i*** when adding these endings (e.g. *happ**y*** → *happ**i**ness*).

1 Can you add suffixes to these adjectives to make nouns? Use your dictionary if needed, especially with the last five.

a	friendly	______	**b**	fair	______
c	honest	______	**d**	forgive	______
e	accept	______	**f**	trustworthy	______
g	obedient	______	**h**	tolerant	______
i	truthful	______	**j**	tender	______
k	thoughtful	______	**l**	loyal	______
m	punctual	______	**n**	generous	______
o	proud	______	**p**	humble	______

2 Add the suffixes ***-ful***, ***-able*** or ***-ate*** to the nouns below to make adjectives.

a	honour	______	**b**	affection	______
c	compassion	______	**d**	charity	______
e	success	______	**f**	joy	______

3 Make up three **true** sentences about yourself or your friends using some of the words in **1** or **2**.

______

______

Dictionary search

We've looked at lots of words about good behaviour, but now let's look at some words about bad behaviour. You have probably heard most of the words below before. Write down what you think they mean, and then check them in your dictionary. If the meaning is different from what you wrote, write it down.

		Your guess	Dictionary meaning
1	rash		
2	impudent		
3	insolent		
4	sullen		
5	boastful		
6	envious		
7	revengeful		
8	conceited		

Read and learn

Have you read any 'cautionary verse'? These are poems written to 'caution' or 'warn' children about how they should behave, and the terrible things that will happen if they don't. The most famous were written by Hilaire Belloc. Like all poems, cautionary verse contains some unusual words or uses them in unusual ways.

1 Read the poem below out loud, with rhythm and expression.

Henry King

WHO CHEWED BITS OF STRING, AND WAS EARLY CUT OFF IN DREADFUL AGONIES

The Chief **Defect** of Henry King
Was chewing little bits of String.
At last he swallowed some which tied
Itself in ugly Knots inside.
Physicians of the **Utmost** Fame
Were called at once; but when they came
They answered, as they took their Fees,
'There is no Cure for this Disease.
Henry will very soon be dead.'
His Parents stood about his Bed
Lamenting his **Untimely** Death,
When Henry, with his Latest Breath,
Cried 'Oh, my Friends, be warned by me,
That Breakfast, Dinner, Lunch and Tea
Are all the Human **Frame** requires ...'
With that the **Wretched** Child **expires**.

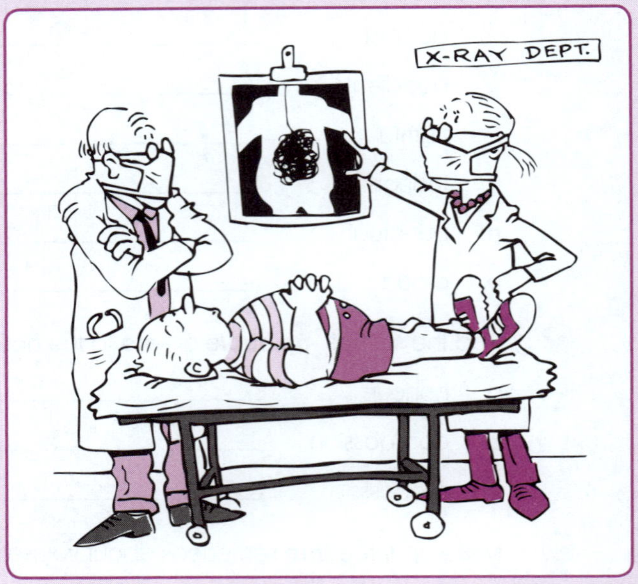

2 Read the poem again closely and then write another word for each of the words in **bold**, using the clues in the text.

a	defect	______	b	physicians	______
c	utmost	______	d	lamenting	______
e	untimely	______	f	frame	______
g	wretched	______	h	expires	______

3 What does 'cut off' mean in the title? ______

4 Why are there so many words with capital letters? *(choose one)*

a They are proper nouns. b It is an old-fashioned style of writing. c They are mistakes.

5 Think about the poem and look at the titles of those in the box above. Then answer the questions by circling the best answer for each.

a Hilaire Belloc wrote poems about ...
 i behaviour that annoys most adults. ii seriously bad behaviour.

b He wrote about ...
 i what usually happens to badly-behaved children.
 ii what could happen to badly-behaved children but probably won't.

c His main purpose was probably to ...
 i amuse children. ii warn children.

Try to find more cautionary verse. Two others by Hilaire Belloc are 'Matilda Who told Lies, and was Burned to Death' and 'Jim, Who ran away from his Nurse, and was eaten by a Lion'. They might not sound like it but they're great fun!

Puzzle

Across

4. This means the same as 9. (8)
5. In the right way. (8)
7. ***Con*** + a school subject. (10)
9. One meaning is 'thinking of others'. (10)
10. We all want this. (9)
13. Synonym of *tolerant*. (9)
15. You can rely on me. (11)
17. A skin colour or quality. (4)
18. ________________ me, I'm sorry. (7)

Down

1. A good feature or characteristic. (7)
2. This means the same as 8. (6)
3. Giving to others. (8)
5. Pre-judging. (9)
6. Faithful. (5)
7. Very brave. (10)
8. Work together. (9)
11. Achieve, win. (7)
12. Goodness. Opposite of *vice*. (6)
14. Farewell. (7)
16. You address a judge as 'Your ________________'. (6)

Your turn to write

Write a poem about the good or bad behaviour of children (one particular child or children in general). If you want, you could try writing cautionary verse using the Henry King poem as your model. Try to use some words from the unit. Be imaginative with your ideas and your language.

☞Answers on pages 160–161

Review 4

Now let's see what you remember of the words you learnt in Units 15–20. There are four tests in this review. You could do all in one session, or you could break them up and do them over a few days.

Step 1 Look at each group of words in the test and memorise them.

Step 2 Cover the five words up and test yourself (column 2). Try to do all five words in one go.

Step 3 Write your score out of 5 in the box. If you got any words wrong, go back and study them again.

Step 4 If possible, ask someone to test you on the words later—an hour or even a day later (column 3).

Test 1

Study	Test yourself	Test with another person
peculiar alien spirit monstrous weird	/5	/5
eerie psychic imaginary extraterrestrial mysterious	/5	/5
behaviour text grotesque unknown perplexed	/5	/5
cemetery phenomenon invisible lonely hoax	/5	/5
athletics shrieks flicks powered force	/5	/5
gear pressure effort vehicle idea	/5	/5
	Total score = out of 30	Total score = out of 30

Test 2

Study	Test yourself	Test with another person
exist fuel forwards automatically nuclear	/5	/5
battery electricity mechanical purpose several	/5	/5
heavy improve because faulty couple	/5	/5
applaud assault audible caution caught	/5	/5
fought law capital mayor naughty	/5	/5
government councillor monarchy federal electorate	/5	/5
	Total score = out of 30	Total score = out of 30

Test 3

Study	Test yourself	Test with another person
premier minister parliament representative participate	/5	/5
political democracy people involved together	/5	/5
although special precious suspicious politician	/5	/5
patient astronomer potential torrential shuttle	/5	/5
satellite essential launch galaxy confidential	/5	/5
collapse eclipse astronaut capsule further	/5	/5
	Total score = out of 30	Total score = out of 30

Test 4

Study	Test yourself	Test with another person
maximum system gravity satellite definite	/5	/5
opposite similarity entire authority forgive	/5	/5
honour curiosity honest truthful value	/5	/5
courageous thoughtful quality knowledge loyal	/5	/5
prejudice guilty generous trustworthy virtue	/5	/5
innocent succeed goodbye properly conscience	/5	/5
	Total score = out of 30	Total score = out of 30

Which word?

1. The spaceship went ________________ than any other had gone before. (*father, farther*)
2. We ________________ the late train. (*court, caught*)
3. There was a ________________ between the two songs. (*paws, pause*)
4. The two leaders talked about how they could achieve ________________. (*peace, piece*)

Congratulations! You've done very well, and learnt a lot about language. Remember: the best way to learn new words is to read, read and then read some more.

☞Answers on page 160

Word list

absolutely
absurd
abundant
abusive
accept
accepting
accessible
accidental
accommodation
accompany
accurate
achievement
active
activity
actually
adaptation
adequate
advance
advantage
adventure
adventurous
advertisement
advice
advisable
aerobics
affect
aggressive
agility
alert
alien
almost
alphabet
already
altar
alter
although
always
ambition
amount
amusing
analyse
ancient
angel
angle
animated
announce
annoyed
answer
answered
Antarctic
anticipate
anxious
apartment
apologise
apostrophe
apparition
appetite
applaud
appreciate
appreciative
apprehensive
apprentice
appropriate
approximate
arcade
archaeology
Arctic
argument
arrest
article
artificial
ask
asked
assault
assistant
asteroid
astrology
astronaut
astronomer
athletics
atmosphere
audible
audience
author
authority
automatically
available
awful
backwards
bakery
balance
ballet
bandage
barrel
battery
because
beginning
behaviour
being
believable
believe
benefit
bizarre
blizzard
board
bored
bought
breath
breathe
brilliant
bronze
building
burden
burglar
burglary
burial
business
busy
cabbage
calamity
calculate
calendar
calm
campaign
cancel
candidate
capable
capital
capsule
captivity
carbohydrates
career
carefully
casual
catastrophe
categorise
caught
cause
caution
cautious
cellophane
cemetery
central
century
certainly
certificate
challenge
champion
chance
channel
character
charity
cheerful
chickenpox
choir
choreographer
chorus
cinema
circle
circulation
circumference
circumstance
citizen
civilised

classical
classics
climax
coarse
collapse
collect
college
comedy
comet
comfortable
comical
commercial
communicate
communication
commuter
compass
competition
competitive
completely
complex
complicate
computerised
concern
concert
conclusion
conduct
conductor
confident
confidential
congestion
connect
connection
conquer
conscience
considerate
consistent
constellation
constitution
construct
contact
contented
context
contradict
controversial
convenient
conversation
convict
cooperate
cottage
council
councillor
couple
courage
courageous
course
court
courteous
create
creature
crevasse
criminal
critically
criticise
curiosity
curious
cutlery
cyberspace
damage
dangerous
data
database
daughter
dazzle
debate
decide
decipher
decision
decisive
defiant
definite
definitely
degree
deliberate
delicate
delicious
democracy
dependent
depot
depth
description
descriptive
desert
deserve
desirable
desperate
despise
dessert
destroyed
determined
devastated
device
devious
devise
diagonal
dialogue
diameter
diary
dictionary
diet
different
difficult
digital
dimension
direct
direction
directory
disadvantage
disappeared
disappointed
disaster
disastrous
discourage
discovered
discovery
disease
disgrace
disguise
disprove
distance
distinct
district
disturb
documentary
dolphin
dosage
double
doubt
drama
dramatise
during
dyeing
dying
dynamite
early
earn
eclipse
ecological
edible
educate
education
eerie
effect
efficient
effort
elect
electorate
electricity
electronic
elegant
eligible
elliptical
eloquent
email
embarrassed
emergency
emotional
emphasise
employment
endangered
endurance
energy
engine
enjoyable
enormous
enough
entertainment
entire
environment
episode
equal

equality
eradicate
escape
essential
estimate
evaluate
evaporate
eventually
evidence
exact
exactly
example
excavation
exceed
excel
excellent
except
excessive
exciting
exercise
exhaust
exhausted
exist
expect
expedition
experience
explain
explanation
explorer
explosive
exquisite
extinct
extract
extraordinary
extraterrestrial
extravagant
extravaganza
extreme
facilities
facility
fact
factories
facts
fair
famous

fantasy
farther
fascinating
fatal
fatigue
faulty
favourite
feat
feature
federal
fictitious
field
film
financial
finite
fireworks
fixes
flexible
flicks
force
forgive
fortunate
forwards
fought
fracture
fragrant
fraud
frequent
friction
frightened
fuel
further
future
galaxy
garbage
gauze
gear
general
generally
generous
genre
geography
ghost
glacier
glamorous

goodbye
gorgeous
government
governor
gradually
granite
graph
graphic
graphics
graphite
gravity
grocery
grotesque
guide
guidance
guilty
habitat
happened
happiness
harbour
haughty
haul
haunted
healthy
hear
heavy
height
here
hermit
hesitant
hexagonal
hideous
hilarious
hoax
honest
honour
horrible
hostage
hostility
humanity
humorous
humour
hurrying
hydrogen
hypocrite

hypothesis
hysterics
iceberg
icy
idea
idle
idol
idolise
ignite
ignorant
illegal
illustration
imaginary
imaginative
immediate
impossible
impressive
improbable
improve
improvise
impulsive
incident
incredible
independent
individual
industrial
infinite
infinity
influence
initial
initiate
injury
innocent
inquisitive
insanity
inspect
inspection
instantaneous
instruct
instrument
intelligent
interactive
interpretation
Internet
interval

intriguing
investigate
invisible
involved
irregular
irresistible
irritated
island
isolate
issue
it's
its
jealous
jewellery
journey
juggle
justice
knowledge
laboratory
language
laugh
launch
law
leakage
learn
lecture
legible
legitimate
leisure
length
limb
liquid
listen
listened
loan
lone
lonely
lose
lovable
loyal
ludicrous
luggage
machinery
magnificent
majority

mall
manage
manufacture
marvel
marvellous
massive
material
materials
maul
maximum
mayor
measure
mechanical
melody
memorise
memory
mercy
mesmorise
message
meteorite
microphone
minimum
minister
miracle
miraculous
mirror
mirth
miserable
misery
missed
mist
mixed
mixture
mobile
mobilise
mockery
model
modernise
monarchy
monstrous
mortgage
motion
multimedia
murder
murky

muscle
musical
musician
mysterious
mystery
mystify
mythical
narrative
naughty
necessary
neighbourhood
nephew
nervous
neutral
next
notice
nought
nuclear
obedient
object
obnoxious
observation
observe
obvious
occupation
occurred
offensive
office
official
opera
opinion
opportunity
oppose
opposite
orbit
orchestra
organise
original
orphan
ought
oxygen
package
pact
palace
parallel

parasite
parliament
partial
participate
passage
passive
patient
pause
peace
peculiar
pedestrian
people
perfect
performance
perimeter
period
permanent
perpendicular
perplexed
persistent
personal
personality
persuasive
pharaoh
pharmacy
phase
pheasant
phenomenon
phenomena
phobia
phonetic
phony
photograph
phrase
physical
physique
piano
piece
planet
pleasant
poaching
poisonous
political
politician
politics

popular
population
possessive
possible
potential
powered
practice
practise
precious
precise
predict
prefer
prefix
prejudice
preliminary
premier
present
pressure
primary
principal
principle
prism
private
probable
problem
procedure
profit
program
project
properly
prophet
protein
proud
prove
psychic
public
punctual
purity
purpose
pyramid
qualification
quality
quay
queue
quiet

quite
racial
rarely
rather
realise
reality
really
reason
reasonable
receive
recognise
recommend
reflect
reflection
reflex
regular
rehearse
reign
relative
relax
relaxation
relevant
reliable
religious
remote
represent
representative
republic
repulsive
research
residential
respect
responsibility
responsible
restaurant
review
revise
rhythm
ridiculous
robbery
romance
rotate
route
sacred
sacrifice

salary
sample
satellite
satisfactory
sauce
saucer
saunter
sausage
savage
scale
scared
scene
scenery
scientist
screen
script
secondary
secret
secretive
security
self-esteem
sensible
sensitive
separate
sequel
serial
series
serious
sermon
service
several
sewerage
shortage
shrieks
shuttle
signal
significant
silence
similarity
simultaneous
since
sincere
site
skirmish
skyscraper

slaughter
social
software
sought
source
special
species
specks
spectacle
sphere
spikes
spirit
spontaneous
squirm
squirt
stalactite
stalagmite
stamina
stationary
stationery
statue
stir
stoppage
storage
storey
story
straight
strait
strange
strength
stretch
structure
struggle
stumble
style
subject
subtract
suburban
succeed
successful
sufficient
sugar
suitable
summarise
summary

supernatural
supervise
supple
suppose
surface
surgery
surly
surprise
surprised
survey
survival
suspect
suspense
suspicious
swerve
swirl
symbolise
symmetrical
symphony
system
talkative
task
taught
technology
telegraph
telescope
temperature
template
temporary
tension
terrain
terrible
territory
terrorise
text
theatre
theatrical
their
theme
theory
there
therefore
they're
thirsty
thoroughfare
thoroughly
though
thought
thoughtful
threatened
through
title
together
tolerance
tomb
torrential
tournament
tragedy
transfixed
trauma
treasure
trek
tricks
triumph
trophy
trustworthy
truthful
tunnel
tunnels
turmoil
unanimous
unique
universe
university
unknown
usage
usually
vacant
vacate
vacuum
valuable
value
variety
various
vehicle
verdict
version
veterinary
vibrant
victory
video
village
vintage
virtue
visual
vitamin
volume
voluntary
voyage
waist
warn
waste
waxing
we're
wear
weight
weird
where
whirl
who's
whose
width
witness
worn
worried
worry
worship
wrong
yore
you're
your

Answers

1 Let's communicate (pages 2–7)

Quick fun (page 2)
1 TELEVISION **2** TELEPHONE **3** TELEGRAPH **4** TELEPATHY **5** TELECAST **6** TELETHON **7** DISTANT **8** Other words you might know: **tele**communication; **tele**conference, **tele**vise, **tele**market, **tele**movie, **tele**text.

Fill in the gaps (page 3)
1 communication **2** signals/messages **3** communicate **4** technology, conversations **5** electronic, email, mobile, messages, instantaneously **6** text **7** Internet, download **8** interactive **9** receive, cyberspace **10** language, interpret

Looking at … *age* words (page 4)
2 **a** package, voyage **b** garbage, cabbage, sausage, sewerage **c** voyage, package, passage, leakage **d** voyage, passage, bandage **e** cabbage, sausage **f** village, cottage **g** usage, dosage,**h** shortage, damage, leakage

3 **a** mortgage **b** vintage **c** hostage **d** savage

4 **a** image **b** voltage/wattage **c** salvage **d** luggage/ baggage **e** percentage **f** beverage **g** plumage **h** forage

Proofreading (pages 4–5)
I'm glad I live in the 21st century. I can't imagine not having telephones and televisions and computers in our homes. It would be very boring to write letters every time you wanted to communicate with someone who was more than a few kilometres away. In films about past times, you sometimes see a person writing a letter, then giving it to someone on horseback to deliver, and then weeks later, receiving the reply from the other person. Nowadays we can send an email or text message and get an answer in an instant, or we can just pick up the phone and our words are sent electronically down the line. It is so easy to have a conversation with anyone, anywhere these days. In the past, they also used to send signals from one town to another using flags and different kinds of message machines. Nowadays, we use satellites in space to bounce signals from one country to another—without wire connections at all. Most of us don't really understand how these communication systems work. We are just glad that they do.

Vocabulary power (page 5)
1 loudly: holler, yell, roar, shriek, screech, cry, bark
softly: sigh, whisper, mumble, murmur, mutter
formally or seriously: announce, declare, state
angrily: snap, hiss, roar, bark
unhappily: sigh, sniff, mutter, moan, groan cry
nervously: blurt, sputter, stammer, stutter
with surprise: gasp, sputter, shriek
about something said or done: remark, observe, comment, add
against something said or done: protest, contradict, complain

2 The best answers are: **a** groaned, moaned, cried **b** announced, declared **c** muttered, mumbled, murmured **d** yelled, cried, blurted **e** remarked, commented **f** stammered, stuttered **g** hollered, yelled **h** hissed, muttered **i** gasped, sputtered, protested

Read and learn (pages 6–7)
1 **a** iii **b** ii **c** i **d** iii **e** i **f** ii **g** iii **h** ii

2 **a** Because wires are used when sending messages by Morse Code.
b Because dashes are used in Morse Code.
c The headline tells us that the contest was close, but Morse Code won.

Puzzle (page 7)
1 **mob**ile (mob) **2** communi**cat**e (cat) **3** sa**tell**ite (tell) **4** inter**active** (active) **5** **mess**age (mess) **6** techno**log**y (log) **7** **data**base (data) **8** Inter**net** (net) **9** **sign**al (sign) **10** **digit**al (digit) **11** langu**age** (age)

2 City streets (pages 8–13)

Quick fun (page 8)
METROPOLITAN: MET, MAN, MEAN, MOAN, MOON, MAIN, MEANT, METRO, TEAM, TERM, TOOT, TRAIN, TRAM, TRAP, TRAIT, TROOP, TRIP, TREAT, RAIN, RATE, RAIL, RANT, ROOT, REAM, ROAM, ROPE, ROTE, PRONE, PRAM, PORT, LEAN, LATE, LAIR, LIT, LAP, LAME, LOITER, LOOP, INTO, POLITE and probably lots more!

Fill in the gaps (page 9)
1 neighbourhood **2** factories, industrial **3** commercial, residential **4** apartments, skyscrapers **5** surburban **6** pedestrians **7** harbours, accessible **8** quay, arcades **9** convenient, facilities **10** vibrant **11** commuter **12** thoroughfare, restaurants, buildings **13** congestion, tunnels

Looking at ... *ant/ent* and *ance/ence* words

(page 10)

1 ***ant* → *ance***: brilliance, ignorance, hesitancy, significance, abundance, elegance, extravagance, fragrance, vacancy, defiance, assistance, relevance
ent* → *ence: presence, dependence, independence, difference, intelligence, confidence, persistence, consistency, obedience, excellence, eloquence, magnificence

2 **a** confident, excellent/brilliant **b** difference **c** magnificent **d** abundance **e** vacancies **f** eloquence/intelligence **g** relevant **h** independence **i** elegant **j** significance

Proofreading

(page 11)

15th May

Today we went into London for the first time. We took the train in with all the commuters going to work and school. I was expecting the central part of the city to be pretty busy, but I couldn't believe just how congested it was with people and traffic. We had to fight our way along the footpaths of the main thoroughfares like Oxford Street and Piccadilly. Everyone was hurrying, weaving in and out and dashing in front of us to get to taxis or buses. Londoners hardly ever wait for the traffic lights or use the pedestrian crossings; they just leap across the roads whenever they see a break. I don't know how they aren't killed.

I was also expecting lots of skyscrapers and modern buildings, but I was wrong about this. Most of the buildings were old. Unfortunately, Mum wanted to visit almost every one of them! Dad wanted to visit the neighbourhood where he grew up, so we took the London underground and came out in a place that was very different—mostly factories and big new office complexes. Dad was disappointed. He said it was all just a quiet residential area when he lived there.

After this, we hopped on a double-decker bus and crawled through the streets. We could see everything! It was excellent.

Vocabulary power

(page 11)

1 **a** CENTIPEDE **b** PEDAL **c** PEDESTAL **d** MOPED **e** IMPEDE **f** PEDOMETER

2 **a** POLICY **b** POLITE **c** POLICE **d** POLITICIAN **e** METROPOLIS **f** COSMOPOLITAN

Read and learn

(pages 12–13)

1 **a** iii **b** i **c** i **d** ii **e** iii **f** iii **g** i **h** ii

Puzzle

(page 13)

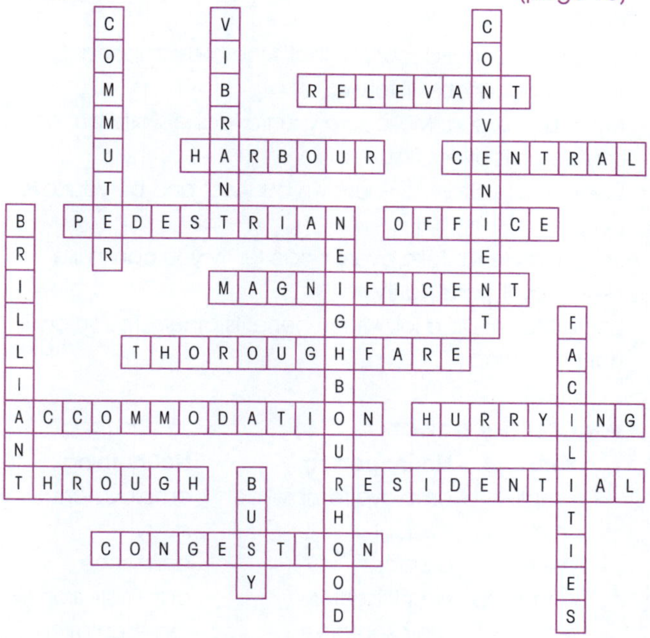

3 When I grow up

(pages 14–19)

Quick fun

(page 14)

1 OPTOMETRIST **2** PILOT **3** MANAGER **4** PHARMACIST **5** JOURNALIST **6** SURGEON **7** ACCOUNTANT **8** BARRISTER

Fill in the gaps

(page 15)

1 casual, degree **2** business, challenging **3** experience, employment **4** ambition, university **5** temporary/casual **6** education, qualifications **7** occupation **8** apprentice, college **9** career **10** permanent **11** financial **12** achievements, future, opportunities/experiences

Killer words

(page 15)

1 SUITABLE CAREER **2** PREFER COLLEGE **3** BENEFIT DEGREE **4** EARN FUTURE **5** REALLY CHALLENGE

Looking at ... *ary, ory* and *ery* words

(page 16)

2 **a** imaginary **b** stationary **c** salary **d** mockery **e** satisfactory **f** cutlery **g** stationery **h** summary **i** misery **j** laboratory **k** mystery **l** directory

3 **a** OBSERVATORY **b** DORMITORY **c** GALLERY **d** ARTERY **e** NURSERY **f** EXTRAORDINARY **g** LITERARY **h** LEGENDARY **i** CENTENARY **j** CONTRARY **k** MONASTERY **l** SECRETARY

Proofreading

(page 17)

I asked my family, friends and neighbours for one piece of advice they would give to young people about choosing a career. This is what they said:

My Mum: Follow your ambition. Do something you love.
My Dad: Choose something in which you can achieve well.
Peter, my neighbour: Do something which challenges your brain.

Aunty Julia: You can be successful without going to university.
My brother Joe: Education: that's the most important thing. A good job will follow.
My cousin Sasha: Make sure you travel the world but get some qualications first.
Uncle Vinnie: Start up your own business and be your own boss.
Johan, a friend: Take every opportunity you can in life. Never say 'I can't do that.'
Uncle Marko: Do a job which benefits others. The salary is not important.

Vocabulary power (page 17)

1

Verb	Noun: person	Noun: thing
employ	employer/employee	employment
study	student	study
assist	assistant	assistance
administer	administrator	administration
represent	representative	representation
manage	manager	management
earn	earner	earning(s)
qualify	qualifier	qualification

2 **a** friendship **b** township **c** membership **d** leadership **e** likelihood **f** fatherhood **g** neighbourhood **h** citizenship **i** childhood

Read and learn (page 18)

1 **a** ii **b** i **c** iii **d** ii **e** ii **f** ii **g** i **h** ii **i** iii **j** ii **k** i

Puzzle (page 19)

1 **a** **car**eer (car) **b** re**ally** (ally) **c** oc**cup**ation (cup) **d** op**port**unity (port) **e** **suitable** (suit, table) **f** p**refer** (refer)
2 **a** collage **b** learn **c** usual **d** agree **e** mature **f** diversity

4 Protecting our wildlife (pages 20–25)

Quick fun (page 20)

1 MAMMAL **2** PRIMATE **3** REPTILE **4** AMPHIBIAN **5** MARSUPIAL **6** ARACHNID **7** MOLLUSC

Fill in the gaps (page 21)

1 species, extinct **2** threatened, disappeared **3** endangered **4** critically **5** habitat, destroyed, territory **6** unique, captivity, research **7** poaching **8** campaign, discourage **9** population **10** diseases **11** responsibility, creatures, ecological, survival

Killer words (page 21)

1 example **2** lose **3** environment **4** gradually **5** facts **6** being

Looking at … homophones (page 22)

1 **a** waist–middle part of the body; waste–rubbish **b** dyeing–changing colour; dying–stopping living **c** missed–past tense of *miss*; mist–fog **d** coarse–rough; course–program **e** warn–advise; worn–past tense of *wear* **f** sauce–food dressing; source–origin **g** alter–change; altar–table used for worship **h** principal–chief, main; principle–rule, policy **i** strait–a narrow stretch of water; straight–direct **j** storey–level; story–tale, narrative **k** except–but for; accept–take **l** caught–past tense of *catch*; court–legal room, sports area **m** mall–shopping centre; maul–claw and bite **n** board–flat, hard piece of wood; bored–uninterested **o** peace–calm; piece–bit, part **p** loan–borrowing; lone– single, one **q** idle–inactive; idol–role model, hero **r** profit–gain; prophet–someone who predicts the future
2 **a** desert–dry land; dessert–sweet
b quite–very, rather; quiet–silent
c breath–air taken into lungs (noun); breathe–inhale or exhale (verb)

Proofreading (pages 22–23)

Some facts and figures about endangered species:

- There are more than 1000 endangered species worldwide.
- Some examples of endangered mammals are the African elephant, the right whale and the blue whale, the gorilla, the tiger and the giant panda.
- There are 800–1000 pandas, including 120 being bred in captivity. Population growth is graduallly destroying their natural habitat: bamboo forests.
- Human beings are the panda's worst enemy. Poachers kill pandas for their skins despite the threat of death or life imprisonment.
- Governments all over the world are doing their best to discourage poaching of many unique species. Two men were caught in China last month after they captured dozens of wild falcons. Because these birds are so rare, huge profits can be made by selling them in other countries.
- Some animals are said to be critically endangered, for example there are fewer than 50 mature Asiatic cheetahs alive—all in one single population in Iran.
- There are many environmental organisations which work hard to protect our planet's wildlife. They do research and run education campaigns. If we don't want to lose more species in the future, we should support these organisations.

Vocabulary power (page 23)

1 **a** DISABLED **b** DISGUISE **c** DISAPPOINT **d** DISCOUNT **e** DISCOVER **f** DISGUST **g** DISPROVE **h** DISADVANTAGE **i** DISQUALIFIED

2 **a** diameter **b** diagnosis **c** enrich **d** surface **e** encircle **f** survey

Read and learn (page 24)

1 **a** ii **b** ii **c** i **d** ii **e** i **f** ii **g** i **h** iii **i** i

Puzzle (page 25)

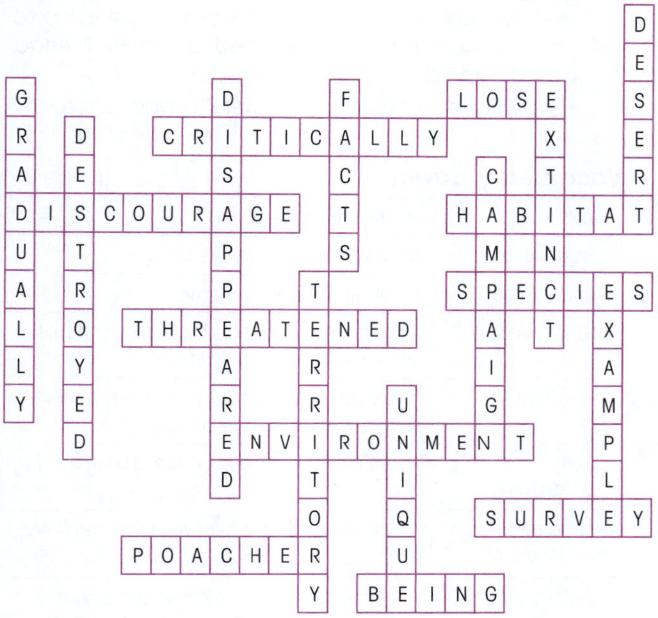

5 For and against (pages 26–31)

Quick fun (page 26)

No correct answers. Answers to American survey given on page 31.

Fill in the gaps (page 27)

1 issue **2** reasons, opinions, oppose **3** believe, neutral **4** evidence, prove **5** various **6** disadvantage **7** serious **8** absolutely/completely, definitely/certainly **9** rarely, arguments **10** deciding, doubt, controversial

Killer words (page 27)

Actually, I'm almost always on time for school, but Lola usually beats me. She's generally in the playground already or in the classroom talking to Ms Pell.

Looking at … *able* and *ible* words (page 28)

1 **a** edible **b** incredible **c** eligible **d** available **e** improbable **f** desirable **g** miserable **h** suitable **i** capable **j** reliable **k** flexible **l** audible **m** legible **n** irresistible **o** sensible **p** advisable

2 **a** PROBABLE **b** BELIEVABLE **c** VALUABLE **d** COMFORTABLE **e** IMPOSSIBLE **f** INVISIBLE **g** TERRIBLE **h** HORRIBLE **i** RESPONSIBLE **j** REASONABLE

Word scramble (page 28)

1 ALMOST **2** DOUBT **3** USUALLY **4** RARELY **5** BALANCE **6** DECIDE **7** VARIOUS **8** SUPPOSE

Proofreading (page 29)

Milo

My team will prove to you that there are many more benefits to living in the country. Kira will talk about the peace and tranquility of the country compared with the congestion and pollution of the city. She will also talk about the advantages of being close to nature and the environment. Jay will tell you about his own experiences living in the country and this real life evidence is sure to persuade you. Without doubt, by the end of this debate, you will have decided that we are correct. Like us, you will want to move to a country town tomorrow.

Matilda

In my opinion, it is certainly better to live in the city than the country. I will give you three very convincing reasons. Firstly it is so much more convenient. You can reach theatres and sports stadiums and museums and galleries very quickly and easily. Secondly, the city is definitely more exciting and vibrant. Every time you walk on the street, you see something interesting. Thirdly, there is generally more opportunity for education and employment. Almost all the jobs are in the big cities. I suppose if you live in the country you might disagree with me. To be honest, I really enjoy visiting the country but I know that on balance I prefer to live in the city.

Vocabulary power (page 29)

2 You might find these words for:

- **a** debate: talk, conversation, discussion, interview and dialogue
- **b** choice: selection, option, preference, alternative, elective
- **c** usual: normal, conventional, orthodox, customary, traditional
- **d** various: diverse, mixed, assorted, miscellaneous, motley
- **e** reasonable (meaning sensible): wise, level-headed, sage, prudent

Read and learn (page 30)

1 **a** iii **b** iii **c** i **d** ii **e** i **f** iii **g** i **h** iii **i** ii **j** ii

Puzzle (page 31)

D	I	S	A	D	V	A	N	T	A	G	E	U	J	A	K
E	S	H	B	C	G	C	A	W	O	E	O	S	Q	R	Y
C	S	B	S	B	V	T	C	U	N	N	P	U	Y	G	A
I	U	M	O	T	N	U	C	D	Y	E	I	A	L	U	R
D	E	X	L	Z	L	A	P	R	A	R	E	L	Y	M	I
E	O	G	U	B	U	L	R	I	D	A	R	L	S	E	O
P	M	A	T	K	F	Y	O	J	H	L	E	Y	R	N	U
Z	H	F	E	F	E	Y	V	D	X	L	F	G	B	T	S
I	S	T	L	A	L	R	E	A	D	Y	M	F	A	B	O
A	J	I	Y	U	T	S	X	E	K	L	D	P	L	B	O
N	D	V	O	H	A	L	W	A	Y	S	V	E	A	E	P
C	O	M	P	L	E	T	E	L	Y	N	K	Q	N	L	P
P	U	R	U	S	X	B	Q	C	R	H	T	W	C	I	O
B	B	Y	J	Q	L	W	S	U	P	P	O	S	E	E	S
F	T	A	V	Y	K	A	C	G	J	M	D	I	Z	V	E
E	M	W	Z	D	E	F	I	N	I	T	E	L	Y	E	X

Review 1 (pages 32–35)

Which word? (pages 34–35)

1 waste **2** quite **3** warn **4** sauce **5** desert **6** strait **7** accept **8** peace

6 Ancient civilisations (pages 36–41)

Quick fun (page 36)

1 WRAP DANCING (rap dancing) **2** A MUMMIFICATION (mummy vacation)

Fill in the gaps (page 37)

1 Archaeology **2** Ancient, hieroglyphic **3** pharaohs, palaces/tombs, embalming **4** religious, worship **5** pyramids, burial **6** Excavation, jewellery, bronze **7** decipher **8** secret **9** treasures **10** sacrifices **11** sacred **12** statues, sites

Killer words (page 37)

1 during **2** conquer **3** eventually **4** period **5** early **6** calendar

Looking at … *ph* words (page 38)

2 **a** trophy **b** phony **c** pheasant **d** triumph **e** catastrophe **f** physique **g** phase **h** phrase **i** phobia **j** graphic

3 **a** sphere, geography, physical

b alphabet, microphone, photograph, telegraph

c phrase, alphabet, phonetic, apostrophe

Proofreading (page 38)

Some interesting facts about ancient Egypt

- The Egyptian civilisation grew up along the banks of the River Nile. In fact, Egypt occupied almost the same area as it does today.
- People's personal possessions were buried with them. Furniture and other household items, jewellery and even food have all been found preserved in tombs.
- People also took images of some animals to their graves—as offerings to the gods.
- Cobras, vultures, hawks, bulls, crocodiles and cats, for example, were considered sacred and worshipped in elaborate religious festivals and ceremonies.
- These animals were given proper burials to please the gods. Many animal cemeteries have been excavated and found to contain mummified cats, dogs, birds and baboons.
- Egyptians believed they could communicate with the gods through the king. The king was thought to be so holy that he could not be referred to directly. Instead he was called 'great house' (or palace)—or in Egyptian *per-o*. From this, we get the word *pharaoh*.

Vocabulary power (page 39)

Word	Meaning in English
bazaar (Arabic)	A marketplace or event like a fete.
mosque (Arabic)	A building for Islamic worship.
zombie (African)	A person brought back to life by magic; a person acting like the walking dead.
icon (Russian)	A holy painting; a famous person who is very special; a computer symbol.
slalom (Scandinavian)	A race around poles and obstacles on skis or in boats.
smorgasbord (Scandinavian)	A variety of food set out for you to choose from.
easel (Dutch)	A wooden frame to hold a picture as it is painted.
smuggle (Dutch)	Take things into or out of a place illegally.
regatta (Italian)	A sports event consisting of boat races.
ghetto (Italian)	A poor city area where one racial or social group live closely together.
grotto (Italian)	A small pretty cave.
karaoke (Japanese)	Singing along with a recording of popular songs for public entertainment.
tsunami (Japanese)	A large, often destructive, sea wave caused by an underground earthquake.
desperado (Spanish)	Someone who does risky, dangerous and perhaps criminal things.

Dictionary search (page 39)

Your dictionary probably said something like:

1 phantom: ghost, apparition, spectre
2 philosopher: thinker, someone who studies truth
3 phoenix: a mythical bird
4 phenomenon: occurrence or circumstance observed (often unusual)
5 phantasmagorical: like a dream or fantasy
6 prophet: someone who speaks for God or sees the future

Read and learn (page 40)

1 **a** ii **b** i **c** ii **d** i **e** i **f** ii **g** ii **h** iii **i** i **j** i **k** i **l** iii **m** ii

Puzzle (page 41)

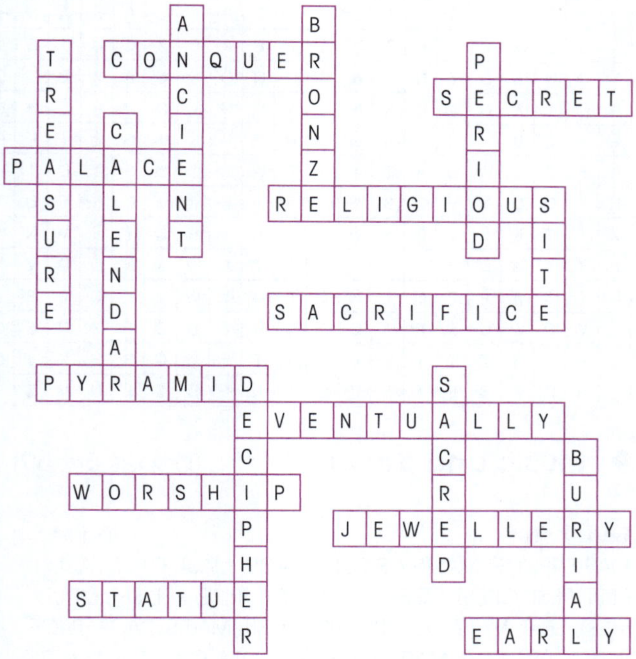

7 Book review (pages 42–47)

Quick fun (page 42)

The Wind in the Willows	Toad Hall
The Wizard of Oz	Emerald City
Alice's Adventures in Wonderland	The rabbit hole
The Adventures of Robin Hood	Sherwood Forest
Hating Alison Ashley	Barranga East Primary
The Lord of the Rings	Middle Earth
Oliver Twist	London
Matilda	Crunchem Hall Primary School
The Lion, the Witch and the Wardrobe	Narnia
Peter Pan	Never-Never Land

Fill in the gaps (page 43)

1 dialogue **2** series, style **3** author/character, genre **4** illustrations **5** exciting/intriguing, adventures **6** themes **7** mysteries, thoroughly **8** atmosphere **9** popular, characters **10** fantasy, fascinating **11** tension, suspense **12** humour, hilarious

Looking at … *ous, ious* and *eous* words (page 44)

2 **a** enormous **b** obvious **c** glamorous **d** curious **e** courageous, famous **f** unanimous **g** generous **h** nervous **i** hideous **j** hilarious, humorous

3 **a** obnoxious, hideous **b** devious **c** simultaneous **d** spontaneous **e** ridiculous/ludicrous **f** marvellous **g** various **h** courteous

Proofreading (pages 44–45)

My favourite book when I was little was *Fantastic Mr Fox* by Roald Dahl, definitely one of the most brilliant authors on the planet. In fact, it is still one of my top five books even though I am now 12. *Fantastic Mr Fox* tells the story of the crafty, wily Mr Fox and three farmers, Boggis, Bunce and Bean: 'about as nasty and mean as any men you could meet'. The three farmers set out to get Mr Fox but they are no match for his cunning and devious mind. Not only is the story hilarious, but the illustrations by Quentin Blake are just marvellous. As well as the four main characters, we meet Mrs Fox and their four children, who all help to outwit the horrible, obnoxious farmers.

I suppose I would say this classic book is most suitable for children aged about 5 or 6 but really I would recommend it to all ages. It has everything: adventure, suspense, tension, great dialogue and wonderful language. Once you start reading, it is impossible to put down. The book makes you respect how animals manage to survive the nasty things humans do to them. However, I don't think this is a serious message. The book is really just fantastic fun.

Vocabulary power (page 45)

1

good	fine, outstanding, enjoyable, excellent
interesting	intriguing, fascinating, enthralling
unusual	surprising, original, bizarre, weird
exciting	thrilling, action-packed, tense, fast-paced, un-put-down-able, gripping
boring	tedious, monotonous, dull, predictable
funny	witty, zany, humorous, amusing, hilarious, comical, wacky
sad	moving, tragic, depressing
real	realistic, authentic, genuine
scary	frightening, spooky, terrifying, nail-biting

Read and learn (pages 46–47)

1 **a** i **b** iii **c** i **d** ii **e** i **f** i **g** iii **h** i **i** i **j** ii **k** ii **l** ii **m** i **n** i

Puzzle (page 47)

1 **sty**le (sty) **2** **ten**se (ten) **3** rum**our** (our) **4** **fan**tasy (fan) **5** the**me** (me) **6** fav**our**ite (our) **7** recom**mend** (mend) **8** though **9** d**anger**ous (anger) **10** various **11** suspense **12** genre **13** **court**eous (court) **14** dialogue

8 How do you feel (pages 48–53)

Quick fun (page 48)

:0—surprised; :–)—happy; :–(—sad; :–||—angry; :–<—very sad; ;–S—confused; :–$—embarrassed; ;–)—only joking

Fill in the gaps (page 49)

1 embarrassed, annoyed/irritated **2** sincerely, determined **3** disappointed, cheerful **4** worried/anxious, emotional **5** surprised, proud **6** jealous **7** frightened, confident **8** calm, anxious/frightened **9** comfortably, contentedly **10** curious

Looking at ... *ive* words (page 50)

2 **a** talkative **b** competitive **c** inquisitive **d** sensitive **e** decisive **f** persuasive **g** aggressive **h** active **i** impulsive **j** imaginative **k** apprehensive **l** impressive

4 **a** excessive **b** narrative **c** relative **d** massive **e** repulsive **f** offensive

Proofreading (page 50–51)

calm	rather	fascinating
proud	worried	laugh
contented	jealous	imaginative
cheerful	disappointed	thought
confident	determined	pleasant
persuasive	emotional	talkative
comfortable	secretive	surprised
frightened	sincere	impressive
curious	embarrassed	hilarious
enjoyable	anxious	strength
annoyed	jewellery	irritated

Vocabulary power (page 51)

1 proud–humble; intelligent–stupid; wise–foolish; enthusiastic–reluctant; joyful–sorrowful; violent–gentle; intentional–accidental; generous–miserly; clumsy–graceful; naughty–well-behaved; secretive–open; calm–anxious; attractive–repulsive; crazy–sane; honest–deceitful; rude–courteous; simple–complex; gloomy–cheerful

2 **a** unpleasant **b** incapable **c** inattentive **d** unsatisfactory **e** harmless **f** unemotional **g** imperfect **h** uncomfortable **i** fearless **j** disobedient **k** disrespectful **l** insensitive **m** disloyal **n** impatient

Read and learn (page 52)

1 Because he has a big pimple. **2** in his room **3** Because porcupines are prickly and sensitive to anyone coming near them (we often say someone is prickly if they get angry easily). **4** Dracula and Wolf Man Because they are scary, and he is scary like them at the moment **5** c **6** He will kill anyone who makes jokes about his pimple; he will cut off their heads and their 'heads will roll' away (He doesn't really mean this of course!). **7** **a** rant **b** guffaw **c** glum **8** **a** as big as a house **b** It will be 'war'.

Dictionary search (page 53)

1 patience **2** sincerity **3** perfection **4** contentment **5** generosity **6** loyalty **7** enthusiasm **8** humility **9** sanity **10** wisdom **11** simplicity **12** anxiety

Puzzle

R	A	P	O	S	S	E	S	S	I	V	E	P	L	E	A	S	A	N	T
A	C	O	M	F	O	R	T	A	B	L	E	R	C	B	C	U	J	G	H
T	O	U	B	G	Z	N	P	N	J	O	Q	O	S	C	A	R	E	D	O
H	M	I	R	O	A	Q	K	N	L	R	M	U	M	D	V	P	L	H	U
E	P	C	B	I	R	U	A	O	D	N	P	D	K	I	G	R	J	K	G
R	E	P	S	W	O	A	T	Y	J	E	A	L	O	U	S	I	D	I	H
H	T	Q	Q	Y	V	U	B	E	M	B	A	R	R	A	S	S	E	D	T
X	I	T	K	P	F	G	S	D	A	S	F	I	E	N	I	E	M	N	W
R	T	I	N	Q	U	I	S	I	T	I	V	E	W	X	N	D	D	V	Y
D	I	S	A	P	P	O	I	N	T	E	D	Y	W	I	C	O	L	F	L
E	V	D	W	O	R	R	I	E	D	U	H	E	U	O	E	X	N	S	G
S	E	C	R	E	T	I	V	E	F	S	T	V	C	U	R	H	X	J	D
L	R	O	X	D	E	T	E	R	M	I	N	E	D	S	E	U	M	Z	T

9 Music and dance (pages 54–59)

Quick fun (page 54)

MASTERPIECE: MASTER, PIECE, PEACE, MAST, CAST, PAST, REST, PEST, CREST, STEP, STEM, STRIPE, TRIPE, PET, SET, MET, MEET, SEAT, MEAT, PEAT, PIE, TIE, PIT, SIT, MACE, RACE, PACE, PART, CART, CAR, MAR, PAR, STAR, PRAM, CRAM, TRAM, STIR, STRIP, TRIP, TERM, PASTE, PAIR, STAIR, PIER, PEER, PEAR, CARE, PARE, MARE, STARE, PESTER, PRICE, MICE, TRICE, RICE

Fill in the gaps (page 55)

1 audience, conductor, orchestra, instruments **2** choir, concert, symphony **3** opera, melody **4** ballet **5** musician, classical **6** musical, chorus **7** performance, theatre **8** popular **9** tunes **10** rehearsed, choreographer **11** extravaganza

Looking at ... *al*, *le* and *el* words (page 56)

1

						C	**O**	M	I	C	A	L			
					S	E	**R**	I	A	L					
				C	I	R	**C**	L	E						
						P	**H**	Y	S	I	C	A	L		
					T	H	**E**	A	T	R	I	C	A	L	
							S	P	E	C	T	A	C	L	E
			C	A	P	I	**T**	A	L						
						P	**R**	I	N	C	I	P	L	E	
P	R	I	N	C	I	P	**A**	L							
				T	I	T	**L**	E							

2 **a** principal **b** principle **c** supple **d** capital **e** punctual **f** spectacle **g** cancel **h** interval **i** dazzle **j** title

Proofreading (page 57)

Musical event of the year

The West in Performance

Civic Theatre, July 20

Featuring: Three student orchestras • 100-strong combined schools choir • Classical, modern and jazz ballet • Musicians and dancers from over forty schools • Popular and classical music — even opera! • Rock and jazz bands • Individual and group performances

Guest choreographer: Jack Bellini Guest conductor: Rose Younan

Don't miss this very special concert. Mark the date on your calendar now!
Tickets available to the public from June 20 Avoid the queue on the night and get front row seats now.
Special prizes for lucky audience members

Vocabulary power (pages 57–58)

1 **a** sound **b** hear/sound **c** see **d** end **e** free **f** place **g** mind **h** carry **i** big **j** lead

2 **a** sounds **b** hearing specialist **c** hearing/ear **d** kept in, limited **e** folder of papers (e.g. drawings) **f** written memories **g** sent out of the country **h** important and powerful person

Read and learn (pages 58–59)

1 a ii **b** i **c** ii **d** i **e** ii **f** i **g** ii **h** i **i** i **j** i **k** ii

Puzzle (page 59)

1 a THEATRE **b** AUDIENCE **c** CONCERT **d** ORCHESTRA

2

Wind instruments	Brass instruments	Stringed instruments	Percussion
flute	tuba	banjo	xylophone
clarinet	bugle	violin	castanets
oboe	trumpet	lute	bongos
saxophone	tuba	ukelele	cymbals
piccolo	cornet	harp	triangle
bassoon	trombone	piano	gong

10 Measuring up (pages 60–65)

Quick fun (page 60)

1 SQUARE **2** TRIANGLE **3** RECTANGLE **4** CIRCLE **5** OCTAGON **6** CONE **7** CUBE **8** CYLINDER **9** SPHERE **10** PYRAMID

Fill in the gaps (page 61)

1 distance **2** circumference, calculated **3** perimeter, symmetrical **4** dimensions, length, width, height **5** hexagonal, depth **6** diameter/diagonal, diagonal/diameter **7** volume **8** weight, accurate, equal **9** measuring, scale **10** prisms

Looking at ... *ate* words (page 62)

1 accurate, adequate, anticipate, appropriate, approximate, candidate, certificate, complicate, considerate, create, debate, deliberate, delicate, educate, estimate, fortunate, immediate, investigate, isolate, legitimate, private, rotate, separate, template, vacate

2 separate, estimate, create, investigate, accurate, approximate, adequate, appropriate, template

3 **a** FORTUNATE **b** TEMPLATE **c** SEPARATE **d** ERADICATE **e** CONSIDERATE **f** APPROPRIATE **g** DELIBERATE **h** CREATE **i** LEGITIMATE **j** DELICATE

Looking at ... measurement words (page 62)

1 cm = centimetre; km = kilometre; kg = kilogram; t = tonne; ml = millilitre; mg = milligram; m = metre; l = litre; g = gram; mm = millimetre

Proofreading (page 63)

- Our group used three dimensional objects to build a tower two metres high.
- We made a large circle in the playground using only two people, a rope and chalk. We then measured the diameter and the circumference.
- We surveyed 20 students to find out how far they thought the school was from the Post Office: about one kilometre, more or less. We then measured it exactly using a trundle wheel, and found only one student got the answer correct.
- Our group planned a fun run in the streets of our suburb and drew a map of the route to scale. Kindergarten to Year 3 will run 500 metres and Years 4–6 will do double that distance.
- We calculated approximately how long the bus trip would take for our excursion, and we were right.
- We each estimated the dimensions of various objects, and then measured them. Each of us got an equal number correct. We were surprised at how accurate our guesses were.
- We experimented with paper planes to find the best model. We varied the weight, length and width of the paper, and the angles of the folds.

Vocabulary power (pages 63–64)

1 **a** triplets **b** quintuplets **c** monopoly **d** decathlon **e** bilingual **f** trilogy **g** quadrangle **h** octopus **i** quadruple **j** triathlon **k** pentagon **l** nonagenarian

2 **a** Pentagon **b** octogenarian **c i** decapod **ii** octopod

Read and learn (pages 64–65)

1 a ii **b** ii **c** i **d** ii **e** ii **f** iii **g** ii **h** i **i** iii **j** i

Puzzle (page 65)

	V	O	L	U	**M**	E						
	D	I	S	T	**A**	N	C	E				
W	E	I	G	H	**T**							
					H	E	I	G	H	T		
					E	Q	U	A	L			
		S	Y	M	**M**	E	T	R	I	C	A	L
			E	X	**A**	C	T	L	Y			
		D	E	P	**T**	H						
				W	**I**	D	T	H				
			A	C	**C**	U	R	A	T	E		
					S	U	R	F	A	C	E	

Review 2 (pages 66–69)

Which word? (pages 67–68)

1 sight **2** site **3** Who's **4** Whose **5** principle **6** principal **7** angel **8** angle **9** scarred **10** scared

11 Reaching the poles (pages 70–75)

Quick fun (page 70)

1 PENGUIN **2** WALRUS **3** SEAL **4** ALBATROSS **5** PETREL **6** SKUA **7** CORMORANT **8** TERN **9** CARIBOU

Fill in the gaps (page 71)

1 extreme, temperatures, blizzards, terrain, glaciers
2 feats, endurance, fatigue **3** journeys, remote **4** route
5 explorer **6** trek, depot **7** territory **8** desert **9** expeditions
10 crevasses **11** compasses

Looking at … soft *c* and *sc* words (page 72)

2 a excel **b** chance **c** excessive **d** advance **e** disgrace **f** decide **g** precise **h** balance **i** cinema **j** announce **k** exceed **l** circumstance

Looking at … apostrophe of possession (page 72)

1 **a** The scientist's achievement was extraordinary. She deserves her award.
b I was allowed to look in the two scientists' diaries.
c The explorer's tale of his lonely Antarctic journey was very moving.
d The survivors' stories of their time underground were truly shocking.
e The rescuers left the men's possessions where they found them.

2 **a** The explorers never met up again.
b The two adventurers could not agree on the best route to take.
c The scientists' families were very proud of their achievements.
d The women's team reached camp before the men's team.
e The dogs stayed with their masters till the end.

Proofreading (page 73)

Antarctica: some fascinating facts

- Amazingly, Antarctica is far drier than the centre of Australia. The average rainfall is just 200 millimetres—less than half the rainfall of Australia and just a little more than the Sahara Desert.
- It is the coldest and windiest place on earth. The temperature can go down to minus 90 degrees Celsius. Winds of up to 320 kilometres regularly blow across the permanent icy cover.
- The continent covers an area of 15.5 square kilometres, but in winter it almost doubles in size.
- Hundreds of scientists live at the Antarctic during the summer months, doing research into global warming, the hole in the ozone layer and the greenhouse effect.
- Its tough terrain and extreme weather conditions have tested the endurance of many courageous explorers over the past century. It has also taken many lives. Robert Falcon Scott's team in 1912 perished on their return journey only 20 kilometres from their food depot.
- It is difficult to say when the Antarctic was actually discovered. Captain Cook saw islands off the coast in 1773, but the first man to set foot on land is thought to be John Davis, an American sealer, in 1821.
- In 1997, an Australian trio reached the South Pole unaided. It was the first Australian expedition to do so, and the fifth ever.

Vocabulary power (page 73)

People: intrepid, heroic, courageous, selfless, inspirational, extraordinary, valiant, gallant, bold, daring, noble
Place: remote, mysterious, desolate, dazzling, harsh, hazardous, magnificent, majestic, sublime
Weather: atrocious, ferocious, raging, abominable, bitter, violent, harsh, freakish, foul, grim, extraordinary

Read and learn (page 74)

1 a ii **b** iii **c** iii **d** i **e** i **f** ii **g** i **h** i **i** ii **j** iii **k** i **l** iii

Dictionary search (page 75)

1 chasm **2** second **3** ***ch*** is pronounced ***k***

Puzzle (page 75)

E	N	D	U	R	A	N	C	E	A	B	B	L	I	Z	Z	A	R	D
X	E	I	S	L	A	N	D	O	X	L	N	U	K	X	A	E	Q	P
P	G	A	F	H	P	Q	E	D	M	T	E	R	R	I	T	O	R	Y
E	U	R	O	U	T	E	S	G	J	P	R	H	G	O	R	Z	O	E
D	V	Y	S	F	E	C	E	D	W	I	A	E	J	K	E	L	U	F
I	B	L	M	O	R	D	R	L	I	D	Q	S	M	I	K	N	T	E
T	E	M	P	E	R	A	T	U	R	E	T	V	S	E	K	W	E	A
I	R	T	T	R	A	F	C	W	Q	P	B	M	F	M	J	A	L	T
O	K	Z	C	S	I	K	E	Z	H	O	X	J	O	U	R	N	E	Y
N	L	N	H	J	N	R	E	M	O	T	E	G	D	Y	Z	M	Y	O
U	S	U	C	C	E	S	S	F	U	L	R	G	L	A	C	I	E	R
A	V	B	D	I	S	C	O	V	E	R	E	D	Y	I	P	A	S	C

12 Health, sport and fitness (pages 76–81)

Quick fun (page 76)

ATHLETICS, SOCCER, CRICKET, BASKETBALL, GYMNASTICS, SWIMMING

Fill in the gaps (page 77)

1 healthier, exercise, regularly/frequently, diet **2** physical, injury **3** competition, leisure, agility **4** limbs **5** sugar, energy **6** stretching, muscles **7** carbohydrates, protein **8** vitamin **9** champion, stamina **10** activities, frequently/regularly

Looking at … horror homophones (page 78)

2 **a** your **b** its **c** Whose, here/there **d** wear **e** their **f** it's **g** We're/They're **h** who's **i** where **j** you're

Word scramble (page 78)

1 STAMINA **2** HEALTHY **3** PHYSICAL **4** STRETCH **5** VARIETY **6** LEISURE **7** CHAMPION **8** ACTIVITY

Proofreading (page 79)

Nina: I like competing in swimming races. When I do well, I feel proud and full of energy.
Susie: Dancing keeps me fit and healthy. If I don't do regular exercise, I feel yucky.
Len: My favourite activities are riding my bike and playing soccer. They're fun.
Suri: I do gymnastics. It's a lot of fun. There is a lot of variety and lots of competitions.
Thea: I play netball. I don't really do it for physical fitness—I do it because it's fun.
Matt: I play soccer. Before each game we stretch our muscles so that we won't get injuries.
Leo: I want to be a champion tennis player, so I don't have much leisure time. I do lots of practice.
Xavier: I do athletics. I like running long distance races best, but I want to improve my stamina.
Anna: I have to eat a balanced diet because I do many sports. Protein and carbohydrates are necessary for me to do well, but so is sugar.
Karl: I don't care who's winning when I race. I just love competing.

Vocabulary power (page 79)

1

Idiom	Meaning
a drag your feet	go very slowly
b lose ground	lose the advantage in a match or competition
c make/gain ground	make progress in a match or competition
d hit your stride	start to do something confidently, after not being so confident
e go ahead in leaps and bounds	improve a great deal
f be home and dry (or hosed)	safely be the winner (even though the competition is not over)
g throw in the towel	give up and stop trying to win
h lose heart	start to feel discouraged because you are not winning
i fight a losing battle	have no chance of winning at all
j win hands down	win very easily
k take the wooden spoon	come last in a competition
l run rings around someone	be much better than the other team or individual
m fight to the bitter end	never give up, even though it looks like you will lose

Read and learn (page 80)

1 **a** rivals **b** appeal **c** strive **d** gruelling **e** blinding **f** soar **g** eager **h** propel **i** agile **j** attained **k** straining **l** lone

2 pain barrier: the point at which pain is too much and stops you doing something (e.g. *It looked like the runner suddenly hit his pain barrier and could not go on.*)
split second: a tiny amount of time (e.g. *Tom beat Jimmy by a split second.*)
underdog: the person or team not expected to win (e.g. *We were the underdogs but we won.*)
personal best: the best time, weight or distance an athlete has done (e.g. *I did my personal best time in the 100 metres last Saturday.*)

Puzzle (page 81)

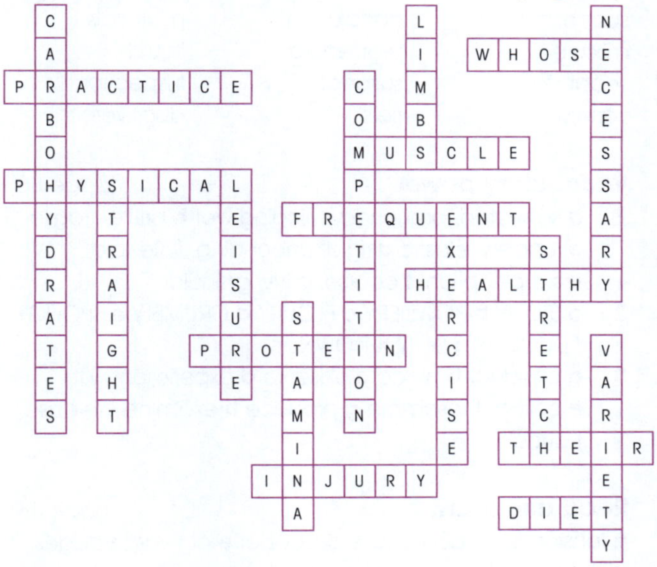

13 Experimenting with science (pages 82–87)

Quick fun (page 82)

1 DATA
DATE
RATE
RACE
RICE

2 TEST
BEST
BEAT
HEAT

Fill in the gaps (page 83)

1 procedures **2** hypothesis **3** investigate, evidence, prove, disprove, theory/theories **4** mixtures **5** surveyed, data, conclusion(s) **6** collect(ed), observ(ed) **7** explains **8** evaporation **9** liquid **10** material, apparatus

Killer words (page 83)

1 CAUSE (inside LIQUID) **2** AMOUNT (inside MIXTURE) **3** TASK (inside THEORY) **4** THEREFORE (inside SURVEY) **5** SEPARATE (inside DATA) **6** CAREFULLY (inside PROVE)

Looking at … *ct* words (page 84)

2 **a** suspect, inspect, fact **b** instruct, lecture, fact **c** predict **d** construct, structure **e** object, convict, verdict **f** reflect, reflection **g** subtract **h** extract

3 **a** extinct **b** directions **c** elections **d** distinctly **e** connected/disconnected **f** unpredictable **g** contradicted **h** verdict/supect

Proofreading (pages 84–85)

disprove	cause	explanation
theory	evaporate	contacts
carefully	amount	task
fracture	collect	objects
predicts	necessary	hypothesis
survey	evaluate	therefore
successful	conclusion	materials
mixture	procedure	liquid
separate	suspect	inspection
variety	field	discovered

Vocabulary power (page 85)

1 **a** saturated, drenched, wringing-wet **b** brittle, fragile **c** rubbery, elastic **d** rigid, unbending, inflexible **e** supple, pliant **f** coarse, gritty, granular

2 **a** STONY **b** POWDERY **c** FLOURY **d** CRUMBLY **e** SPONGY **f** DOUGHY **g** SILKY **h** DOWNY

3 **a** conduct **b** place **c** observe **d** experiment with **e** collect **f** resemble **g** produce **h** examine **i** release **j** attach

Read and learn (page 86)

a tension **b** surface **c** dive **d** pepper **e** outward **f** edges **g** detergent **h** traces **i** properties **j** strong

Puzzle (page 87)

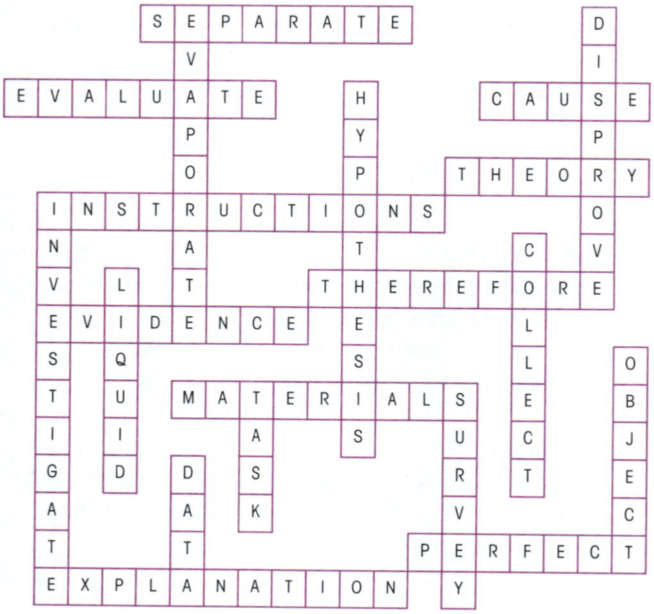

14 When things go wrong (pages 88–93)

Quick fun (page 88)

1 MAN / BOARD = MAN OVERBOARD

2 LOOK KOOL = LOOK BOTH WAYS

3 C YOURSELF YOURSELF YOURSELF YOURSELF = SEE FOR YOURSELF

4 SHUT / SIT = SIT DOWN AND SHUT UP

5 YOUR TIME = YOUR TIME IS UP

6 ON THE ON THE = ON THE DOUBLE

7 LOOK = LOOK OUT

8 WATCH = WATCH OUT

Fill in the gaps (page 89)

1 poisonous, fatal **2** escaped, dangerous, robberies, assaults **3** suspicious, illegal/criminal **4** witness, emergency, arrest **5** disastrous, damage(s), accidental, serious **6** disaster/catastrophe/calamity, problems, difficult

Word scramble (page 89)

1 DAMAGE **2** SERIOUS **3** TRAGEDY **4** ARREST **5** DISASTER **6** ASSAULT

Looking at … *ur, ir* and *er* words (page 90)

2 **a** deserve **b** disturb **c** personal **d** mercy **e** virtue **f** concern **g** Murder **h** stir

3 **a** alert **b** sermon **c** surly **d** mirth **e** turmoil **f** absurd **g** murky **h** skirmish

4 **a** stern **b** dirge **c** quirky **d** curt **e** lurch **f** smirk

Proofreading (pages 90–91)

Last holidays, my family went camping. It was an absolute catastrophe from start to finish. By the end of one week, we were all desperate to get home. I'll go back to day one. The first problem was that a dangerous criminal had escaped that day, and the police were everywhere. They searched every car, and talked to motorists to make sure they knew how seriously dangerous this person was. They asked us to report anything at all that looked suspicious. We were all very frightened, but Mum told us not to worry—she reckoned no one in their right mind would stop our car with four crazy kids in the back and everything but the kitchen sink on top! Anyway we saw nothing (we were quite disappointed actually) and we made it to our campsite near the beach.

Then our real troubles began. First my baby brother trod on a poisonous snake! Luckily the snake was more scared than my brother and it slid away, but from then on, my mother was nervous about every single thing. On the second day, my sister nearly drowned in the surf. She recovered fairly quickly but we took her to the emergency department anyway—an awful experience—worse than the accident itself. All was quiet for two days and then a real disaster struck. The tent fell down … in the middle of the night. Mum said this wouldn't have happened if my father had checked the camping equipment. It only got worse after that. We were all really looking forward to getting back home but then—guess what—the police decided to block all the roads because the prisoner was still at large and had been seen in the area. We did finally get home—after one flat tyre and one fine for illegal parking. I don't think we'll be going camping again for a long, long time.

Vocabulary power (page 91)

1 **a** deep trouble **b** suspicious circumstances/situation **c** prime suspect **d** narrow escape **e** nasty accident **f** unanimous verdict **g** verwhelming evidence **h** man-made disaster **i** convicted criminal **j** armed robbery
k masked bandit **l** tricky situation/circumstances **m** sudden emergency **n** mistaken identity **o** dramatic rescue **p** permanent damage

Dictionary search (page 92)

Illegal act	Meaning	Person who commits act
perjury	telling lies in court	perjurer
manslaughter	killing without intending to	XXXX
vandalism	destroying property for no reason	vandal
extortion	getting a large sum of money by illegal methods	extortionist
blackmail	threatening to do something harmful unless you get money	blackmailer
treason	betraying your country	traitor
slander	telling lies which destroy someone's reputation	slanderer
arson	setting fire to a property	arsonist

Read and learn (pages 92–93)

1 **a** arms and legs going round and round in a wild way **b** a very loud and very deep voice **c** with no control of arms or legs, like a doll made of cloth and stuffing **d** moving arms without really knowing what he was doing or why
2 **a** a rodeo rider of wild horses **b** a strong pole or post, usually made of concrete or metal **c** a sailing boat **d** a sea creature (it belongs to the dolphin family)
3 **a** ii **b** i **c** ii **d** i **e** ii **f** iii

15 Movies and television (pages 94–99)

Quick fun (page 94)

ENTERTAINMENT: TEN, TAN, TIN, TINT, TENT, TIME, TAME, TIRE, TAINT, TIER, RENT, RAM, RAN, RAT, RANT, MATE, MANE, MARE, MAIN, MIRE, MITE, MINE, MEANT, MINT, TINT, TRAIN, RAIN, REAM, TEAR, TRIM, TRAM, TREE, TREAT, MEN, MANNER, MATTER, ENTER, TIMER, ATTIRE (dress), AIM. Did you find any others?

Fill in the gaps (page 95)

1 script **2** feature, screen, guide **3** animated **4** documentary, sequel **5** amusing, romance, comedy **6** drama, original, versions **7** Channel, episodes, reality **8** program, review **9** multimedia, visual

Looking at … *ise* words (page 95)

2 **a** revise, memorise, despise **b** emphasise, memorise **c** realise, recognise, disguise **d** devise, revise, criticise **e** recognise, disguise **f** dramatise, summarise, revise
3 **a** improvise **b** analyse **c** mobilise **d** mesmerise **e** Modernise **f** symbolise **g** idolise **h** categorise

Vocabulary power (pages 96–97)

1

a	**b**
adore	loathe
love	detest
admire	cannot stand/bear
be fond of	hate
enjoy	dislike
like	do not care for

2 very strong approval: unforgettable, inspiring, memorable, awe-inspiring, outstanding, brilliant
strong approval: excellent, strong, classy, clever, impressive, terrific
approval: fine, capable, able, competent, good

Proofreading (page 97)

March of the Penguins
Beautiful filmed documentary follows the incredible journey of the Emperor penguins as they trek across Antarctica to their traditional breeding grounds. Recommended for all the family.

Lassie
Remake of the 1943 original. A family financial crisis forces Joe to sell his beloved collie dog, Lassie, but the faithful dog escapes her new master and makes her way back to Joe. Take your tissues.

The Chronicles of Narnia
Based on the classic novel by CS Lewis, this feature film tells the tale of four children who travel through a wardrobe to the mystical land of Narnia and discover it is their destiny to free the land. Brilliant art direction and special effects.

Charlie and the Chocolate Factory
A young boy from a desperately poor family wins a tour

through the biggest and best chocolate factory in the world, guided by the weird and wonderful Willy Wonka. Wacky humour, bizarre characters and outstanding performances. Sure to be a movie favourite for years to come.

Read and learn (page 98)

1 **a** ii **b** i **c** iii **d** i **e** i **f** i **g** ii **h** iii **i** ii **j** i

2 **a** The word *prequel* means a film/book that shows what happened before the events of an existing film/book. *Pre* means before and *quels* is part of the word *sequels* (a film or book that shows what happens after the events of an existing film/book).

b The word *trilogy* means a series of three books, or films or other works of literature. The prefix **tri-** means three.

Puzzle (page 99)

1 **a** DIRECTION **b** PRODUCTION **c** CASTING **d** SPECIAL EFFECTS **e** SCRIPTWRITING **f** EDITING **g** CINEMATOGRAPHY **h** SOUND **i** LIGHTING **j** PROPS

2 **a** sc**rip**t (rip) **b** ani**mat**ed (mat) **c** re**view** (view) **d** d**ram**a (ram) **e** **document**ary (document) **f** am**us**ing (us) **g** **feat**ure (feat)

Review 3 (pages 100–103)

Which word? (pages 102–103)

1 desert **2** route **3** feat **4** diaries **5** practise **6** we're **7** your **8** their **9** It's

16 Strange happenings (pages 104–109)

Quick fun (page 104)

1 THEY SEE **2** DETECT THIEVES **3** ELEVEN PLUS TWO **4** I'M A DOT IN PLACE

Fill in the gaps (page 105)

1 stranger, behaviour, imaginary **2** Extraterrestrial, Alien **3** mystified/astonished, bizarre/peculiar/weird **4** eerie **5** haunted, apparition, monstrous, grotesquely **6** supernatural **7** phenomena, mysterious **8** psychic, spirits, weird/bizarre/peculiar

Looking at ... the *x* sound (page 106)

2 **a** text, climax, context, prefix, classics **b** relax, flexible, reflex, aerobics, athletics **c** perplexed, transfixed, hysterics, shrieks

3 **a** hoax **b** fixes **c** climax **d** shrieks **e** flexible **f** transfixed **g** graphics **h** complex **i** reflex **j** relax **k** next

Vocabulary power (pages 106–107)

1 **a** blood **b** boots **c** sweat **d** wits **e** dumb **f** daylights **g** nerves **h** pants **i** edge **j** mouth

Proofreading (page 107)

The Unknown

Spooks, spirits, strange and eerie things
Imaginary or real? I don't know. Do you?
Sometimes at night, lonely in my room upstairs,
with the wind blowing and the rain on the windowpanes,
I'm sure they could exist.
But when the sun shines the next morning: forget it. No way.
Then visiting weird old Mrs Fogarty's house on the hill,
near the old cemetery,
I think again. Yep. I'm ready to believe
It's haunted with all sorts of monstrous things.
Sure to be ghosts in the bedrooms. Aliens even.
Probably grotesque monsters too.
But back home, playing footy out the back: no. All
imaginary. Silly me.
Then I catch Mum watching *Supernatural Tales* on the telly.
A very peculiar look on her face. Extraordinary.
She looks almost green. Mmm. Maybe.
Then 'Make me a cup of tea, darling' she calls.
Back to the real world again.
Hey, what's that shrieking noise? Probably an owl.
But I might take my torch up to bed tonight anyway.
Just in case.

Read and learn (pages 108–109)

1 **a** pulsing **b** sheen **c** affliction **d** shudder/quiver **e** involuntarily **f** dimly

2 sea anemone, jelly, slug

3 No correct answer, but most likely answers are: pathetic, afraid, eerie, grotesque, sad

4 moan; because it seems to be alive

5 slowly; with difficulty; wheeze is the sound people make when breathing with difficulty (for example if they have asthma)

6 The boy fainted.

Puzzle (page 109)

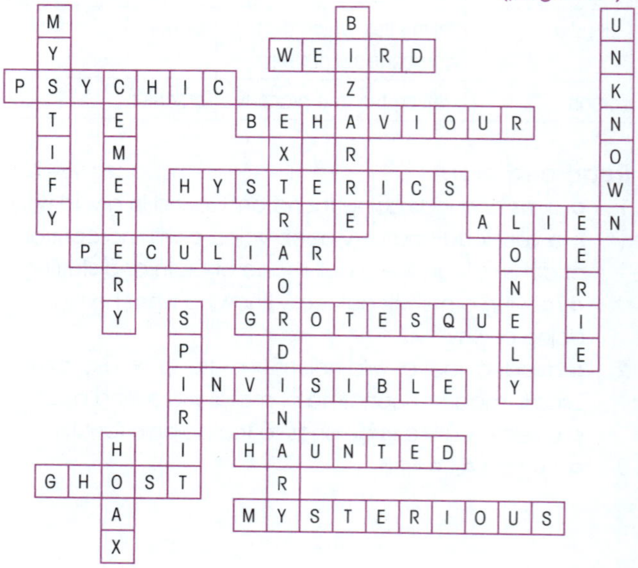

17 Machines and inventions (pages 110–115)

Quick fun (page 110)

1 HERE COME DOTS **2** TO SEE PLACE; **3** REPEATING 'HELLO' **3** THE CLASSROOM

Fill in the gaps (page 111)

1 effort **2** idea **3** device, mechanical **4** computerised **5** force, motion, forwards, backwards **6** fuel, gears **7** pressure **8** Industrial, powered, engine **9** manufacturing, automatically **10** electricity, battery **11** vehicles **12** Nuclear

Looking at ... *au, augh* and *ough* words (page 112)

1 a ought **b** assault **c** slaughter **d** launch **e** haunted **f** cause **g** faulty **h** fraud **i** pause **j** caution **k** audible **l** saucer **m** naughty **n** nought

2 a past tense of seek **b** clap/cheer, approve **c** proud, snobbish **d** walk slowly without care **e** pull **f** bad experience

Proofreading (pages 112–113)

mechanical	effort	computerised
powered	vehicle	engine
pressure	cause	backwards
couple	faulty	automatically
device	thought	purpose
idea	improve	pause
unknown	heavy	caution
several	daughter	behaviour
peculiar	invisible	audible
force	battery	

Vocabulary power (page 113)

1 wellingtons **2** bloomers **3** Braille **4** Celsius, Fahrenheit **5** diesel **6** watt **7** volt **8** pasteurisation **9** sandwich **10** boycott

Read and learn (page 114)

1 **a** ii **b** i **c** ii **d** ii **e** iii **f** iii **g** i **h** ii **i** i **j** iii

2 Androids and humanoids are robots that look and act like humans. You could say the image of the robot in the first paragraph is an android/humanoid. The robot referred to in the last paragraph—driving the car and popping to the shops—is definitely an android/humanoid.

Word scramble (page 115)

1 VEHICLE **2** PRESSURE **3** ELECTRICITY **4** FORWARDS **5** BACKWARDS **6** POWERED **7** MECHANICAL **8** INDUSTRIAL

Puzzle (see answer at bottom of page) (page 115)

18 Governing the country (pages 116–121)

Quick fun (page 116)

1 PARIS **2** ATHENS **3** LONDON **4** ROME **5** HANOI **6** CAIRO **7** BANGKOK **8** MADRID **9** BEIJING **10** BEIRUT **11** KABUL **12** MOSCOW **13** CANBERRA **14** France, Greece, The UK, Italy, Vietnam, Egypt, Thailand, Spain, China, Lebanon, Afghanistan, Russia

Fill in the gaps (page 117)

1 government **2** councils, councillors, Mayor **3** electorate, Premier **4** federal, capital **5** monarchy, constitution, republic **6** representative, Governor, Minister **7** democracy, participate, Parliament **8** political **9** laws, justice

Looking at ... *ti* and *ci* words (page 118)

2 **a** ancient **b** partial **c** special **d** artificial **e** fictitious **f** initial **g** cautious **h** precious **i** essential **j** sufficient

3 **a** delicious **b** potential **c** precious **d** initiate **e** torrential **f** efficient **g** special **h** official **i** racial **j** financial **k** confidential **l** appreciate

Puzzle (Unit 17, page 115)

IMPROVE
POWERED
DEVICE
COUPLE
PURPOSE
PRESSURE
ROBOT

EXIST
SEVERAL
VEHICLE
HEAVY
AUTOMATIC
MECHANICAL
COMPUTER

Dictionary search (page 118)

1 MALICIOUS **2** CRUCIAL **3** PROFICIENT **4** DEFICIENT **5** VICIOUS **6** ASSOCIATION

Read and learn (pages 118–119)

1 **a** invented (a word) **b** have the right **c** be an official **d** special, privileged **e** population **f** even so **g** grew and developed **h** had a responsibility to do something **i** voting secretly **j** watched **k** usual practice **l** people having different views about an issue

Proofreading (page 120)

Our class travelled to our national capital, Canberra, last week to learn about government and politics. We visited many different places but the most interesting was Parliament House. It was very exciting to be standing in the actual building where the Prime Minister, Leader of the Opposition and ministers work and make important decisions on our behalf. We first went into the Great Hall, where many official functions and special social events are held. I thought it was absolutely beautiful, especially the extraordinary tapestry of the Australian bush. We then walked to the House of Representatives and the Senate. The guide explained the different purpose of the two chambers and pointed out where everyone would sit. We met the federal representative for our electorate, Mrs Karen Brinker, and she talked to us about how bills were passed to change laws. She also discussed the opportunities people had to participate in the process of government in a democracy, beginning with voting at elections—at federal, state or local council level. Although we did more fun activities on other days, I enjoyed this day the most. It made me appreciate how many people were involved in running the country and how much work they do.

Vocabulary power (page 120)

2 **a** CIVILIAN **b** CIVILISED **c** SENSIBLE **d** NONSENSE **e** PREDICT **f** DICTATOR **g** REGAL **h** REGIMENT **i** CAPTAIN **j** CAPITAI **k** REVOLVE **l** REVOLT **m** UNITE **n** UNIQUE **o** POPULAR **p** POPULATION

Puzzle (page 121)

C	A	T	C	O	G	O	R	S	P	S	K	S	O	F	F	I	C	I	A	L
O	M	A	O	H	K	F	A	T	J	R	S	E	S	H	E	D	X	O	P	Y
U	A	I	U	S	Q	F	Y	O	R	W	E	X	Z	T	J	E	P	F	P	G
N	Y	U	N	B	J	I	C	G	V	Z	R	M	D	N	K	M	A	V	R	W
C	O	F	C	I	U	G	X	E	I	D	V	V	I	U	U	O	R	L	E	M
I	R	E	I	B	S	P	T	T	C	F	I	A	G	E	T	C	T	P	C	C
L	P	O	L	R	T	T	W	H	W	L	C	O	F	I	R	R	I	V	I	A
P	S	A	L	R	I	B	E	E	P	Q	E	U	H	R	R	A	C	E	A	P
A	Q	C	O	M	C	U	W	R	E	P	U	B	L	I	C	C	I	M	T	I
P	Y	Q	R	Q	E	M	A	Y	U	E	F	I	E	J	V	Y	P	O	E	T
A	C	O	U	N	C	I	I	C	P	O	L	I	T	I	C	I	A	N	W	A
R	E	L	E	C	T	O	R	A	T	E	E	F	V	C	L	K	T	A	A	L
L	S	R	E	R	E	P	R	E	S	E	N	T	A	T	I	V	E	R	L	I
I	S	I	G	O	V	E	R	N	M	E	N	T	F	D	C	Q	K	C	T	N
A	E	N	N	N	P	R	M	X	H	Y	F	E	D	E	R	A	L	H	H	V
M	N	H	Y	D	E	Q	D	O	W	T	C	P	V	M	O	Z	P	D	O	O
E	T	M	P	S	O	Y	L	G	M	P	J	P	S	O	C	I	A	L	U	L
N	I	F	E	D	P	L	E	I	K	A	Y	E	L	Z	J	N	T	I	G	V
T	A	D	Z	J	L	F	V	U	G	R	R	A	M	P	C	D	I	M	H	E
O	L	A	W	P	E	A	C	E	D	L	Z	F	M	A	A	E	E	O	G	D

19 Out in space (pages 122–127)

Quick fun (page 122)

1 SPACE	**2** MOON	**3** MARS
SPARE	MOAN	CARS
STARE	MEAN/MOAT	CANS
STARS	MEAT	CANE
SCARS	HEAT	CONE
SCARE		
SCORE		
SCOPE		

Fill in the gaps (page 123)

1 universe **2** telescopes, astronomers **3** gravity **4** constellation **5** galaxy, system **6** hydrogen **7** eclipse **8** asteroids, meteorites, comets (in any order) **9** collapse **10** astronauts **11** Planets, orbit, elliptical **12** capsule

Looking at … *ite* and *ity* words (page 124)

1 appetite, authority, charity, curiosity, definite, dynamite, equality, exquisite, facility, favourite, finite, granite, graphite, hostility, humanity, hypocrite, ignite, infinite, infinity, insanity, meteorite, opposite, parasite, personality, purity, satellite, security, similarity, stalactite, stalagmite

2 **a** granite **b** graphite **c** parasite **d** stalactite **e** insanity **f** infinite **g** curiosity **h** dynamite **i** definite **j** exquisite

3 **a** hypocrite **b** hostility **c** humanity **d** finite

Proofreading (pages 124–125)

Facts and figures about space

- There is now one less planet in our solar system. In 2006, the world's scientists decided that Pluto did not qualify as a planet.
- There are no limits to the Universe. It is just that we don't have telescopes powerful enough to observe it all.
- Our galaxy, the Milky Way, has more than 200 million, million stars.
- Humans have always looked to the skies, but the Greeks were the first astronomers to record their observations.
- The first astronaut in space was a Russian, Yuri Gagarin, on April 12 1961.
- Our sun looks like the biggest star in our solar system, but that is only because the other stars are much farther away.
- To break earth's gravity, space shuttle engines need to generate more power than 140 Boeing 747 aeroplanes.
- The word satellite means attendant and refers to both natural and man-made bodies that orbit others in space.
- We think of solar eclipses as unusual, but they actually occur somewhere on the planet about once every six months.

Vocabulary power (page 125)

1 **a** astronomic(al) **b** astrological **c** meteoric **d** atmospheric **e** orbital **f** galactic **g** telescopic **h** planetary **i** dynamic **j** nuclear **k** elliptical **l** global **m** robotic **n** gaseous **o** heavenly **p** gravitational

2 **a** SOLAR **b** LUNAR **c** STELLAR **d** SONIC

3 heavenly

Dictionary search (page 125)

1 **a** minute, microscopic, infinitisemal, minuscule, diminutive **b** colossal, gargantuan, mammoth

3 **a** tiny, petite (for a woman), etc. **b** huge, elephantine, enormous, etc.

Read and learn (pages 126–127)

2 **a** monitoring **b** exterior **c** atrophy **d** pellets **e** rehydrated **f** beverages **g** monotonous **h** cramped **i** noxious **j** rodents **k** indefinitely **l** exhalation **m** prospect

Puzzle (page 127)

1 **a** **orb**it (orb) **b** ec**lip**se (lip) **c** sa**tell**ite (tell) **d** **shut**tle (shut) **e** **cap**sule (cap) **f** uni**verse** (verse) **g** co**met**/**met**eorite (met) **h** pla**net** (net) **i** **gala**xy (gala) **j** teles**cop**e (cop) **k** maxi**mum**/mini**mum** (mum) **l** **fur**ther (fur) **m** sy**stem** (stem)

2 **a** launch (take *a* away and you get *lunch*) **b** farther (take *r* away and you get *father*) **c** asteroid (take *a* away and you get *steroid*)

20 Behaving well … and not so well (pages 128–133)

Quick fun (page 128)

ROT, RAT, RAN CAR, TOR (big hill), CORE, TORE, LORE (old custom), TEAR, NEAR, CARE, REAL, RATE, RACE, RANT, REACT, TRACE, LEARN, TREACLE. The nine-letter word is TOLERANCE.

Did you have any others? Remember: they must contain the letter ***R***.

Word scramble (page 128)

1 VIRTUE **2** HONOUR **3** HONEST **4** CHARITY **5** FORGIVE **6** GENEROUS **7** TRUTHFUL **8** PREJUDICE

Fill in the gaps (page 129)

1 charity **2** cooperate, fair **3** guilty, honest, truthful **4** conscience **5** thoughtful, generous **6** qualities/virtues, forgiving **7** trustworthy **8** value **9** loyal **10** honour **11** tolerant, accepting **12** prejudice, knowledge

Looking at … apostrophe review (page 130)

1
- **a** Nelson's family is getting ready for a big party.
- **b** He's been very sick for two weeks and probably shouldn't go, but he doesn't want to miss it.
- **c** It's a really big occasion—his grandparents' sixtieth wedding anniversary.
- **d** All his cousins and his cousins' cousins will be there.
- **e** He will meet his grandfather's brother for the first time.
- **f** His three aunties and uncles from Darwin will be there. They haven't even met Nelson's little brothers.
- **g** His youngest sister's favourite person in the whole world will be there. She's coming all the way from Perth.
- **h** The party will be held at his grandparents' house in Adelaide. It's a long way to travel for most people but they're all coming.
- **i** There'll be a jumping castle for the little children, but the older children will have to help out with serving food and drinks.
- **j** Nelson hasn't seen his grandparents for three years, so it's important to them all that he attends.

2 **a** DOESN'T **b** HASN'T **c** HAVEN'T **d** DIDN'T **e** SHOULDN'T **f** WEREN'T

Proofreading (page 130)

calm	rather	fascinating
cooperate	courageous	thoughtful
quality	knowledge	honour
honest	fair	loyal
properly	charity	prejudice

value	generous	they're
virtue	conscience	system
several	happiness	learn
truthful	haven't	tolerance
further	collapse	definite
forgive	acceptance	succeed

Vocabulary power (page 131)

1 **a** friendliness **b** fairness **c** honesty **d** forgiveness **e** acceptance **f** trustworthiness **g** obedience **h** tolerance **i** truthfulness **j** tenderness **k** thoughtfulness **l** loyalty **m** punctuality **n** generosity **o** pride **p** humility

2 **a** honourable **b** affectionate **c** passionate **d** charitable **e** successful **f** joyful

Dictionary search (page 131)

1 careless, foolish **2** cheeky **3** rude, disrespectful **4** bad-tempered, sulky **5** talking about yourself, showing off **6** wanting what others have **7** wanting to harm someone that has harmed you **8** thinking very well of yourself

Read and learn (page 132)

2 **a** fault **b** doctors **c** greatest **d** regretting **e** too early **f** body **g** miserable, poor **h** dies

3 killed

4 **b**

5 **a** i **b** ii **c** i

Puzzle (page 133)

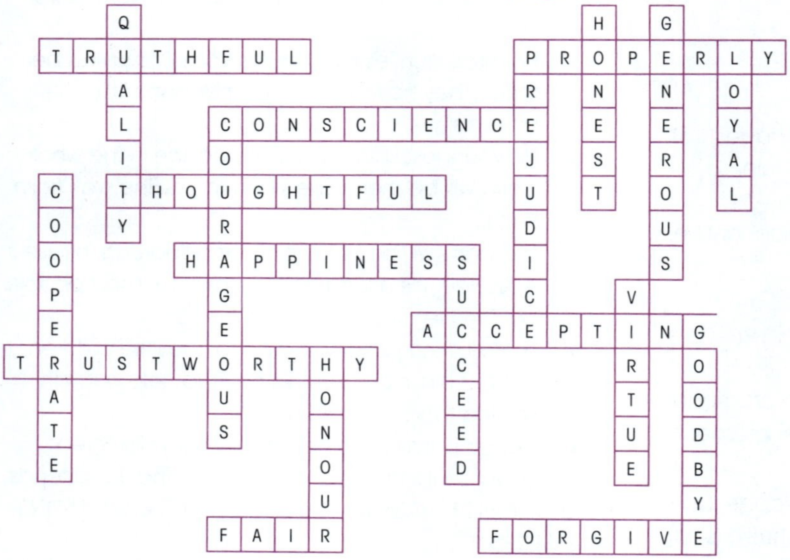

Review 4 (pages 134–137)

Which word? (page 137)

1 farther **2** caught **3** pause **4** peace